Planning and Designing High Speed Networks Using 100VG-AnyLAN

Hewlett-Packard Professional Books

Planning and Designing High Speed Networks Using 100VG-AnyLAN

Janis Furtek Costa

Hewlett-Packard Company

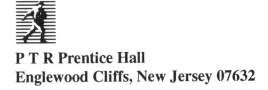

P T R Prentice Hall
Englewood Cliffs, New Jersey 07632

Costa, Janis Furtek.
    Planning and designing high speed networks using 100VG-AnyLAN /
Janis Furtek Costa.
      p.   cm.
    ISBN 0-13-168685-2
    1. Local area networks (Computer networks)--Planning.   I. Title.
II. Title: 100VG-AnyLAN.
TK5105.7.C689 1994
004.6'8--dc20   94-13868
                                                          CIP

Editorial / production supervision: *Mary P. Rottino*
Cover design: *Whitman Studio, Inc.*
Cover illustration: *The Image Bank, Stock Illustrations, Alec Hitchins*
Buyer: *Alexis R. Heydt*
Acquisitions editor: *Karen Gettman*
Editorial assistant: *Barbara Alfieri*

Published by P T R Prentice Hall
Prentice-Hall, Inc.
A Paramount Communications Company
Englewood Cliffs, New Jersey 07632

The publisher offers discounts on this book when ordered in bulk quantities.
For more information, contact:

Corporate Sales Department
P T R Prentice Hall
113 Sylvan Avenue
Englewood Cliffs, NJ 07632
Phone: 201-592-2863,
FAX: 201-592-2249

Printed in the United States of America
10 9 8 7 6 5 4

ISBN 0-13-168685-2

Prentice-Hall International (UK) Limited, *London*
Prentice-Hall of Australia Pty. Limited, *Sydney*
Prentice-Hall Canada Inc., *Toronto*
Prentice-Hall Hispanoamericana, S.A., *Mexico*
Prentice-Hall of India Private Limited, *New Delhi*
Prentice-Hall of Japan, Inc., *Tokyo*
Simon & Schuster Asia Pte. Ltd., *Singapore*
Editora Prentice-Hall do Brasil, Ltda., *Rio de Janeiro*

Contents

4   Bridging and Routing Technology and Network Design

Preface

Is your network feeling the strain of too many users, too little bandwidth, distributed file systems and time-sensitive applications on networks that were designed for data communications only? Are your Ethernet and Token-Ring networks that were once able to handle network traffic now a critical bottleneck in the successful day-to-day operations of your organization? If you woefully answered 'yes' to either question, and you want to know how to improve the performance of your network, then this book is for you.

You will learn what the 100VG-AnyLAN technology is, and determine whether it can increase the performance of your LAN. And if you decide to update your LAN, you will also learn *how* to do it using 100VG-AnyLAN. Practical design recommendations and topology rules are included. Also included is integrating 100VG-AnyLAN with existing technologies, such as cross-point switching and routing.

Networks are rapidly changing. New networking technologies and applications are emerging that virtually obsolete networks of yesterday. With organizations downsizing to PCs and workstations, hardware becoming cheaper and more accessible, and interoperability becoming more and more important, keeping up with your network can be overwhelming. This book can help you update your network with 100VG-AnyLAN.

Acknowledgments

I would like to thank Martha Lopez, Gary Enos, and Catherine Curtis for their contributions— Martha's eye for aesthetics and her help getting the manuscript ready for print, Gary's artistic talent, and Catherine's support, were continuous throughout the development of this book. Without them, this book would not have been.

A special thanks goes out to Kimmi Costa—her patience and understanding during the writing of this book will forever be special to me.

1

Do You Really Know Your Network?

Twenty years ago, computer networks were primarily used for data communications. As PCs began to populate the desktop, local PC user applications such as word processing, spreadsheets, and database programs began to proliferate. Over the last ten years, the advent of fast, lower-cost PCs presaged dramatic growth in computing power and accessibility. With faster PCs and the shift to client-server-based networks with distributed file systems, Ethernet and token ring networks that were once sufficient to handle network traffic became strained. Today, network performance has become a critical bottleneck in many key business application areas such as distributed systems, data-intensive networked applications, and time-sensitive applications. And with the number of nodes in an enterprise doubling every 20 months, the design of your network is crucial to the success of your business.

Is your network congested?

Many corporate network managers admit that their networks may be experiencing network problems, but do not know whether the problems are attributed to chronic network congestion.

Your network may be experiencing network congestion if your users experience:

- variable network response times

- slow networked application operation—slow loading and running

- problems logging onto a network

- network time-outs

- unexpected and abrupt closure of network or server connections

- components not able to access the ring and ring resources in a token-ring environment

- problems accessing or using a network server other than the main network file server, such as database, fax, communication or print server.

Using your network management application, you may also notice these signs of network congestion:

- Peak loads on an Ethernet network exceeding 50%

- Average utilization rates on a 10 Mbit/sec . Ethernet network exceeding 15%

- Collision rates on an Ethernet network exceeding 5%

- Peak utilization rates on a token ring network exceeding 80%

- Average utilization rates on a token ring network exceeding 50%

If you suspect network congestion, review your network. Look at:

- **The physical and logical architecture of your network.** Re-examine network hardware, topology, and protocol usage. Verify (or update) the floor and wiring plans. Update, if necessary, the number and types of PCs and workstations on your network, how each of the PCs and workstations attach to your network, the way your network is segmented, and the number and type of internetworking devices on your network.

- **The way your networks are being used (or abused).** Include the number of users accessing your network and when they use the network (for example, do your users exercise the network more in the afternoon, or at month-end?). Know what operating systems or protocols your users rely on, and the type of applications— note network-intensive applications such as database access and time-sensitive data. Also obtain user feedback on network usage.

- **The future growth of your network**. Integrate the new additions to your network.   Identify potential additions to your network that may impact the network congestion even more.

If you choose to update to a new technology, make the migration and support of a new technology as easy as possible—for yourself and for your users. When considering ways of adding bandwidth to your network, be sure to:

- **Protect your users when upgrading.** The move to a new technology should be as transparent to the user as possible. Your users expect to preserve their software investments and to experience minimal downtime.

- **Preserve as much of your original cable investment as possible**—including the to-the-desk and backbone cables. The cost of pulling new cable may be prohibitive to your budget and user productivity.

- **Look for a solution that follows an industry standard so you don't get locked into one vendor's solution**—the days of proprietary networking protocols are over. Don't let a vendor take control of your network!

- **Build supportability into the network.** Investigate how network management fits into the upgrade. Be comfortable that you can support the upgrade with existing or easily obtainable network diagnostic tools.

Ethernet Congestion

Ethernet Characteristics

Ethernet is a half-duplex, probabilistic (non-deterministic) technology. An Ethernet end node cannot simultaneously receive and transmit information. When one node is accessing the Ethernet network, all other nodes must be in receive mode. When two or more signals exist on the LAN (for example, two nodes transmitting data at the same time), a collision results. After a collision, each end node involved in the collision waits a random amount of time, and then re-transmits its information onto the LAN. The non-deterministic operation of Ethernet networks can be efficient—especially in a lightly used network —but as the amount of traffic increases, collisions increase, and performance drops.

Access to the Ethernet network is a game of chance—when an Ethernet end node wants to transmit, it listens for traffic on the LAN. If traffic does exist on the LAN, the end node continues to listen until the LAN is free of traffic, and then the end node transmits its data. Since there is no central control of traffic, it is probable that, after hearing no traffic on the LAN, two or more end nodes transmit data simultaneously, causing a collision.

Because non-switched Ethernet throughput is limited by its half-duplex technology and its lack of traffic control, the throughput of a 10 Mbit/sec non-switched Ethernet segment will never exceed 10 Mbits/sec—and it is possible that the throughput of a highly utilized network will be a fraction of 10 Mbit/sec. As users are added to the network, the 10 Mbit/s bandwidth must be shared among all users. Busy Ethernet networks begin to experience performance degradation at about 40-50% peak utilization and about 15% average utilization—resulting in unacceptably long response times and unhappy users.

Common Causes of Ethernet Congestion

Network performance problems are usually due to the number of end nodes on a single segment and the type of transactions they are trying to complete. Your network may be congested if you have:

- **High-speed devices jeopardizing the accessibility of the network.** High speed devices, such as servers and workstations, can monopolize the network—causing severe performance problems.

- **Too many users on a single-shared segment.** Too many users on a single-shared segment can have the same effect as a few high-speed devices—network monopolization and degraded throughput.

- **Network-intensive applications.** Since only one end node can access the network at a time, a network intensive application can use the entire bandwidth of the network—for a very long time—resulting in slow network response time.

Possible Solutions to Ethernet Congestion

You can relieve 10 Mbit/sec Ethernet congestion by:

- migrating to faster networks, such as the 100 Mbit/sec 100VG-AnyLAN network

- adding parallel, switching networking capabilities to your Ethernet network

- segmenting your Ethernet network with bridges or routers

Token Ring Congestion

Token Ring Characteristics

By definition, token ring is deterministic—each station on the ring is guaranteed an opportunity to transmit data at regular intervals. Only the station holding the three-byte token is allowed to transmit data onto the ring. The token circulates around the ring, in an idle state, until a station wants to transmit data. The station waits to receive the token, and then transmits its data. If a node's MAC address matches the source address of the packet, it removes the packet from the network. When the originating station is through transmitting, it removes anything that it added to the token frame, and passes the token back onto the ring. Because only the station holding the token can transmit data, token ring networks never experience collisions.

With the introduction of Early Token Release (ETR), available on 16 Mbit/sec token rings, a station releases the token immediately after transmitting a frame. Other stations can append additional frames onto the token—and the additional frames take a free ride around the ring. When the frame arrives at the destination station, it reads the frame without stripping it off the ring. The sending station strips the frame off the ring when it goes by.

Common Causes of Token Ring Congestion

Network congestion occur on a token ring network for the same reasons they occur on an Ethernet network. However, unlike Ethernet, you can make full use of the token ring bandwidth even when many stations are contending for the LAN because no collisions can occur on a token ring network. Ethernet's bandwidth drops off as collisions increase. As utilization increases, the time each station has to wait for the token increases. At 80% utilization, a station's time to transmit a frame onto the ring might double because of the wait time to receive the token.

Congested Network Examples

The following two network examples will be used throughout the book. Each network is typical of its kind—and all may show signs of network congestion during the day. At the peak of the day, the networks may be performance headaches.

Example 1: An Engineering Department

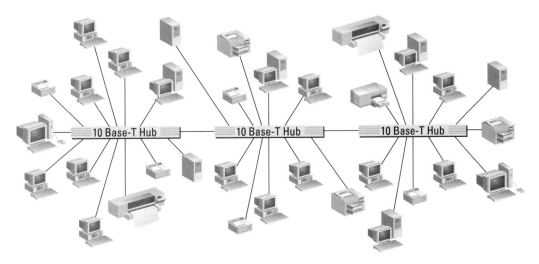

Figure 1-1

This engineering department consists of a clerical staff, hardware development engineers, and software development engineers—with a mixture of PCs and workstations in an Ethernet environment. Most of the PCs on the network are 486-based, and are used by the clerical staff for data base management, word processing, and financial analysis. The engineers also use a few of the PCs to access the company LAN. The workstations are used exclusively by the engineering staff. Applications most commonly used by the workstation users include CAD software, compilers, and circuit simulation software. Approximately 50 users populate the network daily.

Congested Network Examples

The following are key requirements of this network:

- The network must be highly reliable. All files must be accessible, at any time of the day and night, by any engineer on the team.

- File transfers between a user and a server, and between one user and another user, must be blindingly fast. Currently, the engineers are not happy with file transfer times— they feel the large, single burst file transfers are sluggish and damage their productivity. The engineers transfer files often, and are frustrated by the long file transfer delay times.

- The network topology must be simple. The network manager does not want to spend very much time on troubleshooting and maintaining the network.

- The network must respond with minimal delay. All PC applications are networked— the clerical team measures the success of their network by the network response time. The variable network response time currently being experienced by the clerical team is, in their words, "unproductive and unacceptable".

Example 2: Large Insurance Company: Records and Claims Headquarters

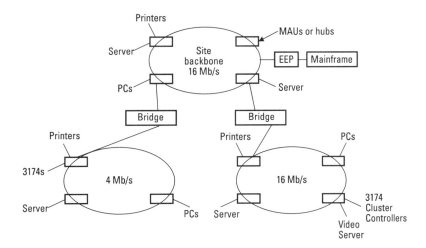

Figure 1-2

The users in this insurance company use 486-based PCs, in a token ring environment. Applications most commonly accessed by the insurance agents include data-base management and multi-media applications (imaging and video for documentation on insured items, and voice for agent annotation). Approximately 100 local users populate the network daily.

The following are key requirements of this network.

- The network must be highly reliable. All files must be accessible, at any time of the day and night, by anyone on the network.

- Must efficiently run multi-media applications—that is, data that is time sensitive, and guarantees bandwidth for the applications that require it.

Congested Network Examples

The networks illustrated above can be upgraded to increase network performance. Whether you add a faster pipe (100VG-AnyLAN), more lanes (cross-point switching), or traffic filters (bridging or routing), performance will be affected.

This book is focused on 100VG-AnyLAN technology, 100VG-AnyLAN network design, and how 100VG-AnyLAN can increase the performance of your network. It also discusses other technologies that will enhance 100VG-AnyLAN networks, such as

- cross-point switching and

- bridging and routing

By the end of this book, you will be able to describe 100VG-AnyLAN, and design an optimal 100VG-AnyLAN network.

2

100VG-AnyLAN Technology
and Network Design

Overview

100VG-AnyLAN is based on the emerging IEEE 802.12 standard for transmitting IEEE 802.3 Ethernet and IEEE 802.5 token ring frame information at 100 Mbits per second. This chapter describes 100VG-AnyLAN design and technical considerations—information you can use to give you a head start in planning for 100VG-AnyLAN networks.

100VG-AnyLAN brings together the best characteristics of Ethernet and token ring— combining the simple, fast network access familiar to Ethernet users, with the strong control and deterministic characteristics of token ring technology.

100VG-AnyLAN technology supports network design rules and topologies of Ethernet 10Base-T and token-ring networks. 100VG-AnyLAN is designed to run on existing Ethernet and token ring cable infrastructures. If your cable meets the 10Base-T or token ring cable specifications, then it will work for 100VG-AnyLAN networks— you will not need to alter your existing network design and cabling when you upgrade to 100VG-AnyLAN's higher transmission speed.

100VG-AnyLAN also offers message-frame compatibility with IEEE 802.3, Ethernet, and IEEE 802.5 token ring networks. You do not need to change existing network operating systems and user software applications when you upgrade or add 100VG-AnyLAN to your network. Because of frame type compatibility, you can connect your 100VG-AnyLAN network to any existing IEEE 802.3, Ethernet, and IEEE 802.5 token ring network with a simple bridge. 100VG-AnyLAN may also be routed to FDDI and ATM backbones and wide area network (WAN) connections.

100VG-AnyLAN uses a centrally controlled access method referred to as the Demand Priority Protocol (DPP). This access method is a simple, deterministic request method that maximizes network efficiency by eliminating network collisions and token rotation delays. In addition, the demand priority protocol uses one level of priority for data and another level of priority for multi-media, so each user request is guaranteed access to the network for emerging time-critical multi-media applications such as real-time video teleconferencing or interactive video.

100VG-AnyLAN Network Components

The 100VG-AnyLAN network is defined as a physical star topology consisting of:

- one or more 100VG-AnyLAN hubs (repeaters)

- two or more 100VG-AnyLAN end nodes

- network links

- optional internetworking devices, such as routers, bridges, and switches.

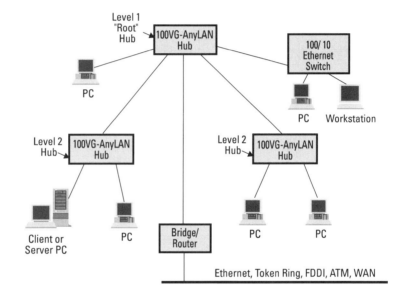

Figure 2-1

The 100VG-AnyLAN Hub (Repeater)

Central to the 100VG-AnyLAN network is the 100VG-AnyLAN hub—also referred to as a repeater. All 100VG-AnyLAN network devices connect to the 100VG-AnyLAN hub. The hub may have two types of ports:

- **Down-link ports** are used to connect 100VG-AnyLAN devices to the network. One down-link port is required for each connected end node or lower level hub.

- The **up-link port** is optional and is reserved for cascading hubs—that is, connecting lower-level hubs to upper level hubs.

You can also protect the security of your 100VG-AnyLAN network with these built-in 100VG-AnyLAN security modes:

- **Private mode** is when an end node or a port on the hub receives only packets specifically addressed to it.

- **Promiscuous mode** is when an end node or a port on the hub receives all packets on the network.

Private and promiscuous modes can be automatically sensed or configured by a network administrator. You may wish to manually configure a down-link port in the promiscuous mode when you troubleshoot your network—this allows network traffic from all communicating ports to be captured with a network analyzer. 100VG-AnyLAN nodes, such as bridges and routers may also request promiscuous operation.

100VG-AnyLAN Nodes

The 100VG-AnyLAN node may be a client or server PC, workstation, or any other 100VG-AnyLAN network device such as a switch, bridge, router or another 100VG-AnyLAN hub.

As with your Ethernet or token ring networks, your 100VG-AnyLAN network can be segmented with the use of bridges, switches, or routers. You can cascade 100VG-AnyLAN hubs within a single subnet without requiring additional bridges or other connecting components. The cascaded hubs are referred to as Level 2 hubs (or 3, 4... dependent on the level of hub); for example, the network in figure 2-1 consists of one Level 1 hub and two Level 2 hubs.

100VG-AnyLAN Network Link

You may use the following cable types in a 100VG-AnyLAN network:

- 4-pair, category 3 (voice grade), unshielded twisted-pair cable

- 4-pair, category 4, unshielded twisted-pair cable

- 4-pair, category 5, unshielded twisted-pair cable

- 2-pair, shielded, twisted-pair cable

- optical fibers

Support of 2-pair, category 5 (data grade), unshielded twisted-pair cable support is currently under investigation

To minimize crosstalk on bundled cable (25-pair binder-groups), your hub should support:

- **Store-and-forwarding.** This allows group-addressed packets to be transmitted to all ports by storing the packet as the end node transmits it, and retransmitting the packet once reception from the end node is complete.

- **Private mode security.** This allows an individually-addressed packet to be transmitted only to the end node to which it is addressed.

100VG-AnyLAN and the OSI Model

The proposed 100VG-AnyLAN standard specifications define standards at the Data Link (Layer 2) and Physical (Layer 1) of the ISO Open Systems Reference Model.

The Data Link Layer (DLL) is comprised of these two sublayers:

- The Logical Link Control (LLC)
- Media Access Control (MAC)

The Physical Layer is also comprised of two sublayers:

- Physical Medium Independent (PMI)
- Physical Medium Dependent (PMD)

Also included in the physical layer is the Medium Independent Interface (MII) and the Medium Independent Interface (MDI). MII is the interface between the PMI and the PMD sublayers. The MII also allows the interchange of PMD layers supporting different links.

The MDI is the physical interface to the medium.

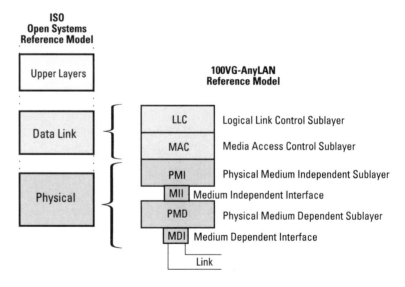

Figure 2-2

OSI Data Link Layer (Layer 2)

The function of the data link layer of the ISO Open Systems
Reference Model (Layer 2) is to ensure reliable transmission
between two nodes. The packet is received from the network layer
(OSI layer 3) to the data link layer, and the data link layer adds the
source and destination address, framing characters, and redundancy
check (CRC) error controls.

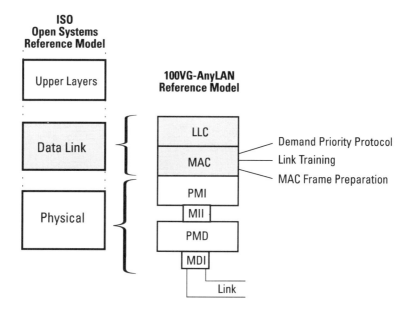

Figure 2-3

100VG-AnyLAN networks support Ethernet-formatted or token
ring-formatted packets. 100VG-AnyLAN Ethernet-formatted packets
support either the Ethernet frame format or the IEEE 802.3 frame
format. If the IEEE 802.3 format is used, the IEEE 802.2 LLC is used
above it. If the Ethernet format is used, there is no LLC sublayer.

OSI Data Link Layer (Layer 2)

The 100VG-AnyLAN data link layer for IEEE 802.3 and IEEE 802.5 is defined as the:

- Logical Link Control (LLC) Sublayer and the

- Media Access Control Sublayer consisting of :

  - Demand Priority Protocol (DPP)

  - Link Training

  - MAC Frame Preparation

Logical Link Control (LLC)

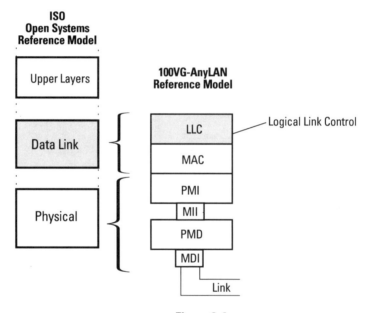

Figure 2-4

The upper sublayer in the 100VG-AnyLAN is typically an:

- IEEE 802.2 Class I LLC supporting Type 1 unacknowledged, connectionless-mode transmission or an

- IEEE 802.2 Class II LLC supporting Type 2, connection-mode transmission

Media Access Control (MAC) Sublayer

When a frame is ready for transmission, the frame is sent from the LLC sublayer to the MAC sublayer, where the appropriate IEEE 802.3-based or IEEE 802.5-based MAC frame is built.

When the data packet is received, the MAC layer verifies the destination address, performs an FCS check on the received frame, and checks whether any other transmission errors have been detected.

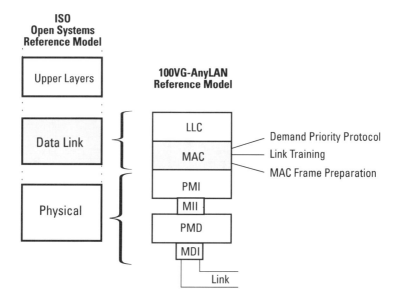

Figure 2-5

Functions of the MAC sublayer in the end node include:
- adding the MAC-specific fields to the frame before sending it to the physical layer (prior to transmission)
- checking received frames for transmission errors
- initiation of control to the PMI
- stripping the MAC-specific fields after receipt from the physical layer, prior to sending it up to the network layer.

Functions of the MAC sublayer in the hub node include:
- accepting transmit requests from end nodes
- interpreting destination addresses
- sending incoming packets to the appropriate outbound ports

The Demand Priority Protocol (DPP)

The Demand Priority Protocol (DPP) is defined by the proposed 100VG-AnyLAN standard as the Media Access Control sublayer (MAC) of the ISO Open Systems Reference Model. DPP defines the process of determining which packet to transmit, and in what order they are processed.

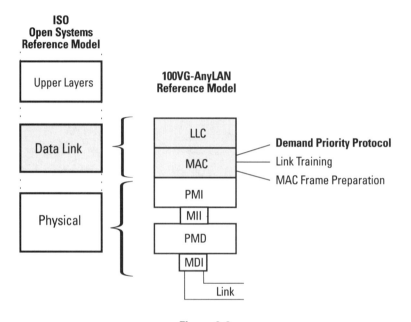

Figure 2-6

If an end node is ready to transmit a packet, it sends a normal-priority request or a high-priority request to the hub. If an end node is idle, it sends idle signals to the hub.

The hub performs a round-robin poll to all of its connected devices to see if any are ready to transmit. A round-robin poll is sequential—a polling cycle begins when the hub polls the lowest-numbered (connected) port. A polling cycle is complete when the highest-numbered connected port is polled. If more than one one node wants to transmit, then the hub determines transmission order based on two criteria:

- the priority (normal or high) of the request

- the physical port order of the end node

For example, suppose the network is idle—that is, the hub is transmitting idle signals to all of its connected and functioning ports, and all of the connected and functioning end nodes are sending idle signals back to the hub. Note that only those end nodes turned on and functioning will transmit idle signals.

The hub polls all of its nodes—including lower-level hubs, and receives idle signals from all of them. When a node wants to transmit a packet, it sends a request to the hub. If an end node is ready to transmit and is connected to a lower-level hub, the lower level hub requests service from its upper-level hub. In this example, only one request is pending from an end node. The hub immediately acknowledges the request from the source end node and the source end node begins transmitting its packet to the hub. As the packet arrives at the hub, the hub decodes the destination address contained in the packet and automatically sends the incoming packet to the outbound destination port(s) and other connected hubs, bridges, and routers.

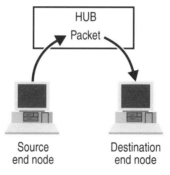

Figure 2-7

If more than one end node requests service from a hub, the hub implements a prioritized, round-robin arbitration procedure to determine what order the packets will be transmitted. The arbitration procedure is based on the port order of the source node and priority level of each packet.

If the end node is ready to transmit, it sends a request to the hub. Each end node can send only one packet per polling cycle.

Each cascaded, lower-level hub (a hub connected to a higher level hub) completes a round robin poll of its own to determine which of its ports want to transmit. If a request is pending from any of its end nodes, the higher-level hub temporarily passes the control of the network to the lower-level hub for packet arbitration. The lower-level hub completes a round-robin poll and sends the requests, one at a time, to the upper-level hub. If more than one request is pending, the lower-level hub issues a request for every end node requesting to transmit. Only one request per end node per polling cycle is allowed. For example, six PCs are attached to a level-two hub, and all six PCs are ready to transmit. Each of the six PCs sends a request to the level-two hub. The root hub temporarily passes control of the network to the level-two hub. The level-two hub completes a round-robin polling cycle, and allows each of the six PCs (in port-order) to send a request to the root hub. Only one packet can be sent by each of the six ports during a round-robin poll cycle.

Each request is assigned a normal- or high-priority designation. High-priority requests are granted access to the network before normal-priority requests—guaranteeing appropriate service for time-sensitive applications such as multi-media applications. The priority designation can be automatically assigned by the user's application or the network manager can configure a port for high- or normal-priority operation. Each hub maintains a separate list for normal-priority and high-priority requests.

After completing the packet transmission currently in process, a hub polls all of its connected ports to determine which have requests pending. If only normal-priority requests are pending, the hub services the requests (in port order) until a high-priority request is received by the hub. After completing the packet transmission currently in process, the hub services that high-priority request. All high-priority requests will be serviced before the hub services normal-priority requests.

Safeguards are built into the proposed 100VG-AnyLAN standard against one or more end nodes marking all of its packets high-priority—thus compromising the performance of the network. To guarantee access for normal-priority requests, a watch dog protocol in the hub monitors all normal-priority requests. Normal-priority requests that have been pending between 200 and 300 ms are automatically elevated to high-priority, and serviced in port-order as indicated by the high-priority request list.

Consider the 100VG-AnyLAN network in figure 2-8.

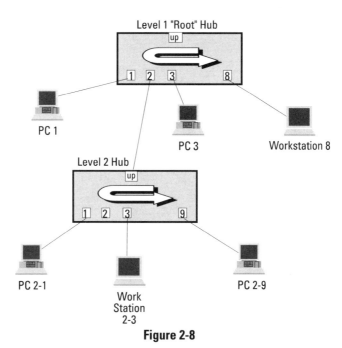

Figure 2-8

Three devices (2 PCs and a workstation) and a level 2 100VG-AnyLAN hub are connected to the root, level 1 hub. Note that a special *up-link* port is used to connect lower level hubs to a port on the root hub. Three single-port devices (2 PCs and 1 workstation) are connected to the level 2 hub.

Use figure 2-8 for the following examples:

Example 1: All ports connected to the root hub have normal-priority requests pending, and the root hub is currently servicing the request from PC 1. Since the hub services all normal-priority requests on a port-order basis, the root hub will process the requests in the following order:

1. *PC 1:* The hub is in the process of servicing its request.

2. *PC 2-1:* Port 2 of the root hub is connected to a second-level hub. When the root hub recognizes Port 2 as another hub, it passes control of the network to the second-level hub for packet arbitration. The second-level hub services its requests on a port-order basis. The first request that is granted is from PC 2-1, since it is the lowest-numbered connected port connected to the level 2 hub.

3. **Workstation 2-3:** The root hub continues to process all of the requests from the second-level hub. The next request (in port order) from the second level hub is from Workstation 2-3, so the root hub processes that request.

4. **PC 2-9:** The root hub continues to process all of the requests from the second-level hub. One more request is pending from the level-two hub's round robin—The request from PC 2-9. The root processes that request.

5. **PC 3:** No more requests are pending from the second-level hub so the root hub takes back control of packet arbitration, and continues the round robin on its ports. The next port-ordered request pending is from PC 3, so the root hub services its request from PC 3.

6. **Workstation 8:** The root hub continues to service requests from the port-ordered round robin—and services the last remaining request pending on the root hub—the request from Workstation 8.

Example 2: All ports except Workstation 2-3 have normal-priority requests pending, and the root hub is currently servicing the request from PC 1. While the root hub is servicing that request, Workstation 2-3 sends a high-priority request to the second-level hub, which it forwards to the root hub. The root hub processes the requests in the following order:

1. **PC 1:** The hub is in the process of servicing its request and will continue to do so.

2. **Workstation 2-3:** Since the second-level hub forwarded the high-priority request to the root hub, and a high-priority request takes precedence over a normal-priority request, the root hub processes Port 2-3's high-priority request before all other normal-requests.

3. **PC 2-1, then PC 2-9, then PC 3, then Workstation 8:** After the hub processes the high-priority request, it continues to process normal-priority requests on a port-order basis.

Example 3: All of the nodes except PC 1 are running very network-intensive programs—and all of the packets originating from these nodes are marked as high-priority. While the root hub is servicing high-priority requests from the high priority users, PC 1 sends the root hub a normal-priority request. While this normally indicates inappropriate use of high priority (many nodes sending all of their requests high priority), safeguards were built into the proposed 100VG-AnyLAN standard to ensure network accessibility to all nodes on the network.

The root hub process the requests in the following order:

1. **High-priority requests (in port order):** The root hub will continue to process high-priority requests from the high-priority end users until the normal-priority request from PC 1 has been pending for 200-300 ms (depending on the configuration of the watchdog timer).

2. *PC 1:* Once the value on the watchdog timer is exceeded, The root hub will:

   a. complete processing the current high-priority packet

   b. change the priority on PC 1's request from normal to high-priority

   c. poll the high-priority request list and determine, using port order, which high-priority request to process .

   d. Process the high-priority request from PC 1 when PC 1's request appears in the high-priority round robin.

3. *Remaining high priority requests:* After processing the request from PC 1, the root hub will continue to process high-priority requests from the four end users.

The network manager, through network management software or other network monitoring devices, should be aware of this situation. If a high number of users continue to mark all of their packets as high-priority, the network manager can configure the hub to treat packets from a particular port as normal priority, regardless of request priority.

Link Training

Link Training is defined by the proposed 100VG-AnyLAN standard as part of the Data Link Layer (Layer 2), Media Access Control sublayer (MAC) of the ISO Open Systems Reference Model.

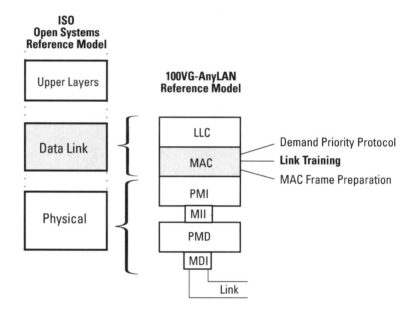

Figure 2-9

Link training is a process that prepares the hub and a connecting end node for communication. Link training:

- verifies the cable between a hub and an end node

- allows the hub to determine the address of an end node

Link training verifies the operation of the link connecting the hub and the node. During link training, the hub and an end node exchange training packets. If link training is successful, data has been transferred between the hub and the end node, and between the end node and hub—thus verifying the cable run between a hub and an end node.

When training is in progress between a hub and an end node, the training frames are passed to all hubs to alert them that training is in process somewhere on the network.

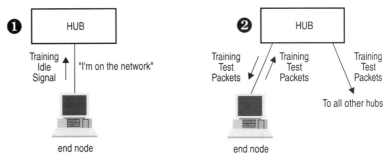

Figure 2-10

Link training also allows the hub to automatically learn information about the end nodes it is connected to. Packets received by the hub from the training node contain information such as:

- the device type. For example, hubs, bridges, and end nodes are identified.

- operational mode (normal or promiscuous)

- MAC-level address (station address) of each end node device

As you can surmise, this level of information can be very helpful when you are troubleshooting the network. Verification of cabling pinouts, MAC-level configuration, and device connectivity is built into 100VG-AnyLAN.

If an end node is attached to a hub, link training is always initiated by the end node when the end node and the hub are first powered on, or when the end node is first connected to the hub. Reinitialization (re-training) may also be performed when transmission error counts or other error conditions reach a predetermined level. Hub-to-hub link training is very similar to end-node link training, and serves to verify the link between the two devices.

MAC Frame Preparation

MAC Frame Preparation is defined by the proposed 100VG-AnyLAN standard as part of the Data Link Layer (Layer 2), Media Access Control sublayer (MAC) of the ISO Open Systems Reference Model.

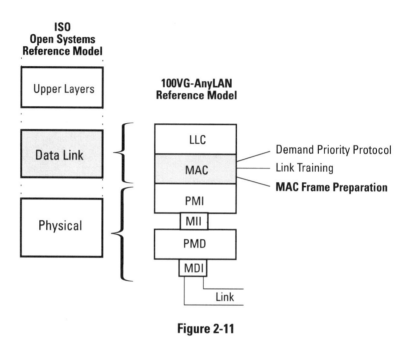

Figure 2-11

Before the packet is sent to the Physical Layer (Layer 1 of the ISO Open Systems Reference Model), these MAC headers and trailers are added to the data packet:

- Padding to complete the data field, if necessary

- Node Destination and Source Addresses

- Frame Check Sequence (FCS)

100VG-AnyLAN MAC Frame

100VG-AnyLAN supports these MAC-frame formats:

- IEEE 802.3-based (Ethernet-type) frames

- IEEE 802.5-based (token ring-type) frames

- IEEE 802.3-based special training packet frames

100VG-AnyLAN networks are assumed to be homogenous—that is, a single-shared (single 100 Mbit/sec domain) 100VG-AnyLAN segment can only support one frame format, and not both IEEE 802.3 Ethernet and IEEE 802.5 token ring frames, at the same time. Conversion between Ethernet and token-ring format is a bridging function. If your 100VG-AnyLAN IEEE 802.3-frame-formatted nodes and your 100VG-AnyLAN IEEE 802.5-frame-formatted nodes need to communicate with each other, a 100VG-AnyLAN Ethernet-to-token-ring bridge is required.

If you wish to attach an existing 10 Mbit/sec Ethernet to a 100 Mbit/sec Ethernet-frame-based 100VG-AnyLAN, or attach an existing 16 Mbit/sec or 4 Mbit/sec token ring network to a 100 Mbit/sec token-ring-frame-based 100VG-AnyLAN, a simple speed-matching bridge is required.

Bit Order in an IEEE 802.3 Frame

The order of the bits, and the way they are depicted in the following illustrations, should be interpreted without ambiguity. The bit order of an 802.3 frame is as follows:

- Data is always illustrated as traveling from right to left—that is, the first bit to be transmitted is illustrated as the left-most bit, and this left-most bit is considered the least significant bit in an octet. The source and destination fields, however, are defined as binary values (and most of the time represented in hexadecimal) and are transmitted as such.

- In a frame, the highest-order octet is transmitted first.

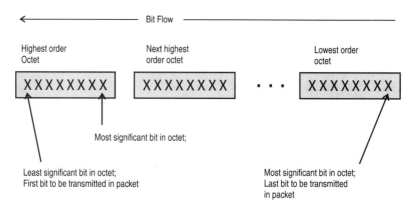

Figure 2-12

Elements of an IEEE 802.3 MAC Frame

The IEEE 802.3 MAC frame is shown below. Note that it is exactly the IEEE 802.3 frame format used in 10 Mbit/sec IEEE 802.3 networks.

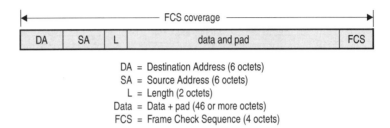

DA = Destination Address (6 octets)
SA = Source Address (6 octets)
L = Length (2 octets)
Data = Data + pad (46 or more octets)
FCS = Frame Check Sequence (4 octets)

Figure 2-13

The Destination Address Field (DA):   This 6 octet (48 bit) address is the hardware address of the intended recipient of the packet. The destination address is further distinguished by the the I/G bit and the U/L bit—the first two bits of the address.

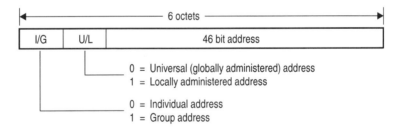

0 = Universal (globally administered) address
1 = Locally administered address

0 = Individual address
1 = Group address

Figure 2-14

Table 2-1 describes the types of 802.3 addresses as indicated by the I/G and U/L bits.

Table 2-1

If the bit settings are	...then this address is:
I/G = 0 and the remaining bits in the address field do not contain all 0s	An **individual address**. An individual address is sometimes called a station or MAC address. It is a physical address uniquely describing an end node. The individual address of a NIC is usually stored in ROM or can be overridden by a network administrator. It is important that no two nodes on your network have the same individual address.
I/G , U/L, and the remaining bits in the address field are 0s	A **null address**. Null addresses are reserved as the destination address in training frames.
I/G = 1	A **group address**. A group address is an address common to a group of users. It is used to address a particular group of end nodes. If the I/G, U/L, and remaining bits in the address field are all 1's, then it is a special group address called a **broadcast address**. A broadcast address addresses all end nodes on a given LAN.
U/L = 0	An address **universally administered** by the IEEE. Every end node on a LAN must have a unique MAC address. The NIC is shipped with a MAC address stored in its ROM—and this address is guaranteed to be unique to all other NICs. A universally administered address signifies that the MAC address supplied on the ROM will be used. For more information about universal address administration, contact: Registration Authority for ISO8802-5 C/O The Institute of Electrical and Electronic Engineers, INC. 445 Hoes Lane P.O. Box 1331 Piscataway, New Jersey 08855-1331, U.S.A.
U/L = 1	An address **locally administered** by a network administrator. The network administrator has supplied the end node's MAC address , overriding the address provided on the ROM. If locally administered addresses are used, care must be taken to assure that all nodes are assigned a unique address. The address must be unique across LANs.

Source Address Field (SA)   This 6 octet (48 bit) address is the hardware address of the end node sending the packet—and is provided by the sender's MAC layer. The source address uses the same format as the destination field—with the I/G bit set to 0.

Length Field   The length field strengthens the error detection capabilities. The length field is specific to IEEE 802.3 frames—the length field is replaced by the "type" field in an Ethernet format packets. The value in the length field corresponds to the number of octets in the data field (not including pads). This field is not required for 100VG-AnyLAN, but is included in the packet for compatibility to 10 Mbit/sec IEEE 802.3 frames.

Data (and optional Pad) Field   The data field consists of the data from a user's application, and all headers and trailers from upper layer protocols. For example, the IP address generated by the IP protocol (IP is a layer 3 network protocol) is considered data by the MAC layer since IP is a upper level protocol. The Data field contains a minimum of 46 octets and a maximum of 1500 octets. If the data in the packet is less than 46 octets, extra octets are added to the end of the data field to bring the total number of octets to 46.

Packets greater than 1500 may be ignored or discarded, or used in a proprietary manner.

Frame Check Sequence Field (FCS)   The 32-bit Frame Check Sequence is used for error detection. A standard algorithm is used to calculate the FCS.

After the packet is transmitted, the data link layer on the destination node re-computes the FCS, based on the packet it just received. The bit values in the transmitted destination address, source address, length and data (and optional pad) fields are used to compute the FCS. It compares that value to the actual FCS value in the FCS field of the packet. If the two values do not match, the data link layer detects the error and the appropriate error detection is completed.

Bit Order in an IEEE 802.5 Frame

The bit order of an IEEE 802.5 token ring frame differs from the bit order of an IEEE 802.3 frame. The bit order of an IEEE 802.5 token ring frame is as follows:

- Data is always illustrated as traveling from right to left—that is, the first bit to be transmitted is the left-most bit, and this left-most bit is considered the most significant bit in an octet. The source and destination fields, however, are defined as binary values (usually depicted in hexadecimal) and are transmitted as such.

- In a frame, the highest-order octet is transmitted first.

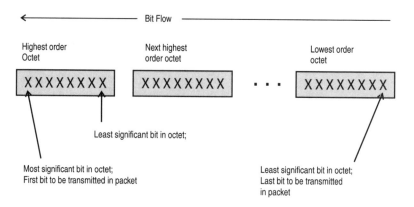

Figure 2-15

Elements of an IEEE 802.5 MAC Frame

The IEEE 802.5 MAC frame is shown below. Note that it is exactly the same IEEE 802.5 token ring frame used in 4 Mbit/sec and 16 Mbit/sec IEEE 802.5 token ring networks.

All information that is IEEE 802.5 token ring specific is only useful if bridging to a IEEE 802.5 token ring network—these fields are not used, but are preserved, in 100VG-AnyLAN networks.

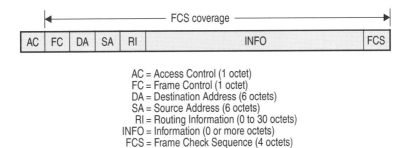

AC = Access Control (1 octet)
FC = Frame Control (1 octet)
DA = Destination Address (6 octets)
SA = Source Address (6 octets)
RI = Routing Information (0 to 30 octets)
INFO = Information (0 or more octets)
FCS = Frame Check Sequence (4 octets)

Figure 2-16

Access Control Field (1 octet)   This field is IEEE 802.5 specific. 100VG-AnyLAN preserves the field for packets bridged to a 4 Mbit/sec or 16 Mbit/sec IEEE 802.5 token ring network. It is not decoded in the 100VG-AnyLAN protocol.

Frame Control Field (1 octet)   The frame control field describes the type of token ring frame and identifies user priority. It is not used in the 100VG-AnyLAN protocol—however, it is preserved for the case where the packet is bridged to a IEEE 802.5 4 Mbit/sec or 16 Mbit/sec token ring network.

Destination Address Field (6 octets)   This 6 octet (48 bit) address is the MAC address of the intended recipient of the packet. The destination address is further distinguished by the the I/G bit and the U/L bit—the first two bits of the address.

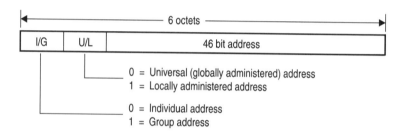

Figure 2-17

Table 2-2 describes the types of IEEE 802.5 addresses as indicated by the I/G and U/L bits.

Table 2-2

If the bit settings are	...then this address is:
I/G = 0 and the remaining bits in the address field do not contain all 0's	An **individual address**. An individual address is sometimes called a station or MAC address. It is a physical address uniquely describing an end node. The individual address of a NIC is usually stored in ROM or can be overridden by a network administrator. It is important that no two nodes on your network have the same individual address.
I/G , U/L, and the remaining bits in the address field are all 0's	A **null address**. Null addresses are reserved as the destination address in training frames.
I/G = 1 and the remaining bits in the address field are not all 1's	A **group address**. A group address is an address common to a group of users. It is used to address a particular group of end nodes. If the I/G, U/L, and remaining bits in the address field are all 1's, then it is a **broadcast address**. A broadcast address addresses all end nodes on a given LAN.
U/L = 0	An address **universally administered** by the IEEE. Every end node on a LAN must have a unique MAC address. The NIC is shipped with a MAC address stored in its ROM—and this address is guaranteed to be unique to all other NICs. A universally administered address signifies that the MAC address supplied on the ROM will be used. For more information about universal address administration, contact: Registration Authority for ISO8802-5 C/O The Institute of Electrical and Electronic Engineers, INC. 445 Hoes Lane P.O. Box 1331 Piscataway, New Jersey 08855-1331, U.S.A.
U/L = 1	An address **locally administered** by a network administrator. The network administrator has supplied the end node's MAC address , overriding the address provided on the ROM. If locally administered addresses are used, care must be taken to assure that all nodes are assigned a unique address. The address must be unique across LANs.

If the bit settings are	...then this address is:
I/G=1, U/L=1 and the next 15 bits are 0	A **functional address**. The first 17 bits of a functional address denote functional addressing, the remaining 31 bits denote separate functional address(es). Examples of types functional addresses denoted by the functional address include: ■ Ring Parameter Server ■ Ring Error Monitor ■ Configuration Report Server If the I/G = 1, U/L = 1, the next 15 bits are 0, and the remaining 31 bits are 1, then it is a special **functional broadcast address**.

Source Address Field (6 octets)   This 6 octet (48 bit) address is the hardware address of the sender of the packet—and is provided by the sender's MAC layer. The source address uses the same format as the destination field—with the I/G bit used instead to denote routing information. The source address may also be either locally or globally administered, as indicated in figure 2-18.

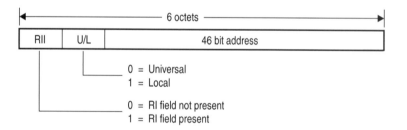

Figure 2-18

Table 2-3a describes the parameters of the source address field.

Table 2-3a

If the bit setting is:	...then
RII = 0	A **routing information** field is not present in this frame.
RII =1	A **routing information** field is present in this frame.
U/L = 0	An address **universally administered** by the IEEE. Every end node on a LAN must have a unique MAC address. The NIC is shipped with a MAC address stored in its ROM—and this address is guaranteed to be unique to all other NICs. A universally administered address signifies that the MAC address supplied on the ROM will be used. For more information about universal address administration, contact: Registration Authority for ISO8802-5 C/O The Institute of Electrical and Electronic Engineers, INC. 445 Hoes Lane P.O. Box 1331 Piscataway, New Jersey 08855-1331, U.S.A.
U/L = 1	An address **locally administered** by a network administrator. Because the token ring address structure is hierarchical , exercise caution when using locally administered addresses. The 14 low order bits of the first two octets of the address are the ring IDs. Two values of ring IDs were assigned for use with all stations: a *null ring*—all zeros, and *Any ring*—all ones. Because of this, care should be taken with the following hexadecimal addresses: 40 00 xx xx xx xx, 7F FF xx xx xx xx, CO 00 xx xx xx xx, and FF FF xx xx xx xx. In addition, locally administered group addresses with the last four octets denoted as hexadecimal FF FF FF FF may also be recognized by hierarchical addressing as a broadcast address.

Routing Information Field (0 - 30 octets) When the RII bit in the source address field is 1, the Routing Information Field is present in the frame. The routing information field is used when the frame must cross a bridge to traverse between multiple rings.

Information Field(0 or more octets)   The information field contains zero or more octets containing ring-management or LLC information. The maximum length of the RI and information fields combined is 4502 octets.

Frame Check Sequence Field (4 octets)   The Frame Check Sequence is used for error detection. A standard algorithm is used to calculate a 32-bit, FCS value based on the values of the frame control, destination address, source address, routing information, info, and data fields.

After the packet is transmitted, the data link layer on the destination node re-computes the FCS based on the packet it just received. It compares that value to the actual FCS value in the FCS field of the packet. If the two values do not match, the data link layer detects the error and notifies the LLC.

Elements of the IEEE 802.12 Training Frame

During link training, special training frames are passed between the hub and the end node. All training frame fields, except for the config field, conform to the IEEE 802.3 MAC frame structure.

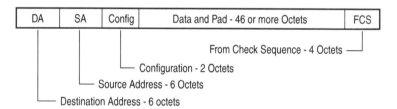

Figure 2-19

Destination Address   The destination address of a training packet is always a null address (all bits are zero).
During link training, the 100VG-AnyLAN hub and an initializing node attached to that hub exchange a series of special training packets. Because a training packet is sent by one specific end node, the destination address is implied as the hub, and the destination address field is not needed.

Training packets are forwarded to all repeaters in a cascaded network. The null destination address identifies it as a training packet, and prevents it from being sent to any end nodes.

Source Address   Link training identifies the source address of an end node:

■ If the end node initiating link training is a PC, workstation, or bridge, the source address is the MAC address (physical address) of that device.

■ If the end node initiating link training is a lower level hub, the source address is a null address unless it contains an integrated network management entity (NME) —it may then pass its MAC address to the upper-level hub.

Configuration   The IEEE 802.3 length field has been replaced with a 16-bit configuration field since the length field is not needed in a training packet. The first four bits of the configuration field are used to provide information about the connected equipment, as shown in figure 2-20 and table 2-3b.

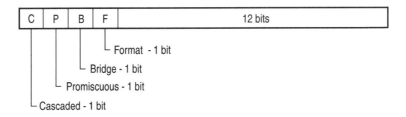

Figure 2-20

Table 2-3b

If the bit setting is:	...then
C = 0	The hub is connected to an end node.
C = 1	The hub is connected to another, lower level hub.
P = 0	The end node is not requesting to be a promiscuous receiver. The end node will only accept packets specifically addressed to it.
P = 1	The end node is requesting to be a promiscuous receiver. A promiscuous receiver can accept all message traffic transmitted on the network. The end node may impose its own filtering, however, and choose to accept all packets or filter out packets.
B = 0	The end node is not a bridge.
B = 1	The end node is a bridge. All packets, except those packets the hub filters, are accepted by a bridge. If the packet is addressed to an end node connected to a hub, that hub will filter the packet (not send the packet to the bridge.
F = 0	Use the IEEE 802.3 format when processing packets from this end node.
F = 1	Use the IEEE 802.5 token ring format when processing packets from this end node.

Data   The training data is 596 octets, each with a value of 0.

Frame Check Sequence   The Frame Check Sequence is used for error detection. A standard algorithm is used to calculate a 32-bit, FCS value based on the values of the destination address, source address, configuration and data fields.

After the packet is transmit, the data link layer on the destination node re-computes the FCS based on the packet it just received. It compares that value to the actual FCS value in the FCS field of the packet. If the two values do not match, the data link layer detects the error and the end node is notified.

Physical Layer (Layer 1)

The function of the Physical layer of the ISO Open Systems Reference Model (Layer 1) is to transfer raw bits between one end node (individual end node, hub, bridge, etc.) and another end node. The physical layer defines procedures and protocols associated with the physical transmission of the bits —for example, cable interfaces, data signal encoding, and connector types and pinouts are specified in the physical layer.

The 100VG-AnyLAN physical layer is defined as the:

- Physical Medium Independent (PMI) Sublayer

- Physical Medium Dependent (PMD) Sublayer

The Medium Independent Interface (MII) interfaces the PMI with the PMD. Another interface—the Medium Dependent Interface is the connector that interfaces the PMD to the cable . Figure 2-21 is an example of an unshielded twisted pair (cat 3) physical layer. Note how the four channels in the PMI layer correspond to the four twisted-pairs of cat 3 UTP cable.

Physical Layer (Layer 1)

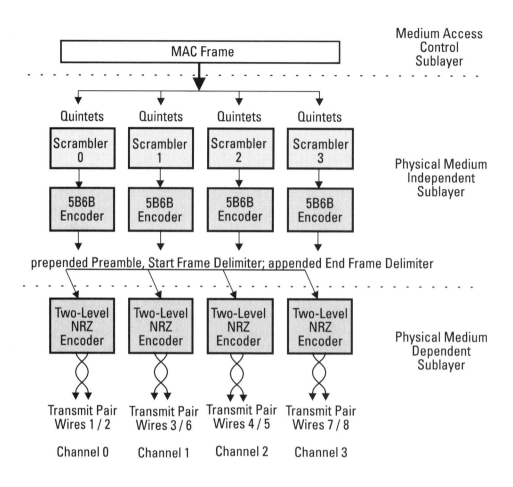

Figure 2-21

The Physical Medium Independent (PMI) Sublayer

The Physical Medium Independent (PMI) sublayer is link independent—that is, the packet will be processed by the PMI layer in exactly the same way, regardless of the medium used in your network.

When the PMI is ready to transmit a packet, it:

- forwards data octets from the MAC layer

- prepares the packet for transmission onto the physical medium

When the PMI receives a packet, it prepares it for the MAC layer by stripping physical layer headers and trailers.

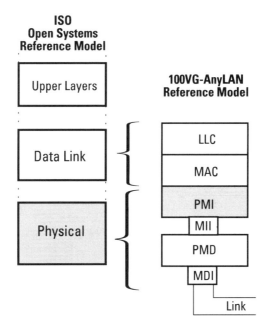

Figure 2-22

Physical Layer (Layer 1)

The PMI functions defined for 100VG-AnyLAN include:

- octet-to-quintet conversion

- data scrambling

- 5B6B encoding

- preamble, SFD and EFD generation

The following figure illustrates the PMI sublayer:

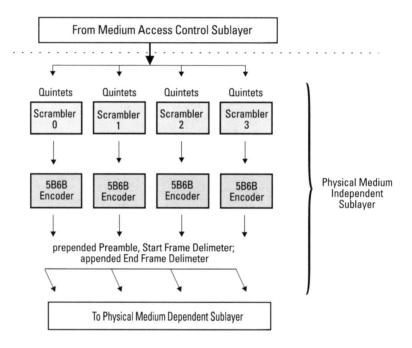

Figure 2-23

Quartet Channeling: Octet-to-Quintet Conversion

Quartet channeling is the process of splitting a single stream of MAC octets into four parallel streams of quintets (5 bit quantities).

Each stream is a called a PMI channel—and in cat 3 UTP, each channel represents a twisted-pair.

Two-pair shielded twisted-pair and fiber optic 100VG-AnyLAN networks use a multiplexing scheme that is described in the section entitled *The Physical Medium Dependent (PMD) Sublayer.*

Data Scrambling

Data Scrambling is the process of scrambling the 5-bit data quintets—using a different scrambling mechanism for each channel—to randomize the bit patterns on each transmission pair. Scrambling each channel eliminates repetitious data patterns such as all 1s or all 0s.

5B6B Encoding (Quintet-to-Sextet Conversion)

Prior to being sent to the physical layer for actual transmission , the scrambled data quintets are encoded into 6-bit sextets, using 5B6B encoding. 5B6B encoding is the process of encoding 5-bit data quintets into predetermined 6-bit symbols. This process creates a balanced data pattern—containing an equal number of 0s and 1s—to provide guaranteed clock transition synchronization for receiver circuitry. 5B6B encoding also provides additional error-checking. Invalid symbols and invalid data patterns (such as more than three 1s or three 0s in a row) are easily detected.

SFD and EFD Generation

Before the packet is sent to the Physical Medium Dependent (PMD) for actual transmission, a preamble, and start-of-frame delimiter is added to the front of the packet. An end-of-frame delimiter is added to the end of the packet.

PMI Function Example

The following two illustrations show the PMI function in a node transmitting data (figure 2-24) and node receiving data (figure 2-25).

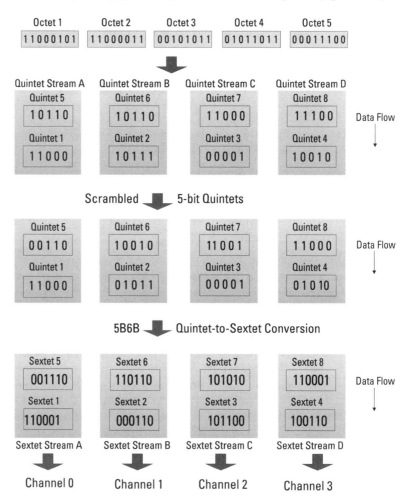

Figure 2-24

Before the sextets are transmitted, a preamble, start frame delimiter, filler bits, and end-frame delimiter are added.

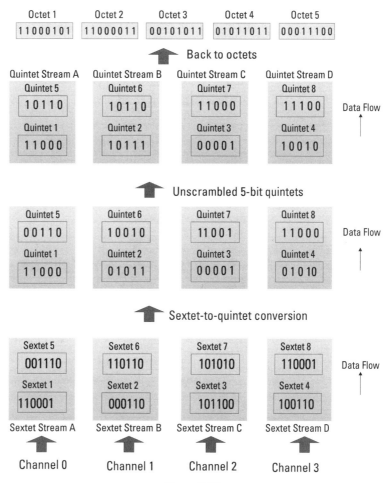

Figure 2-25

The 100VG-AnyLAN Physical Layer Frame

The 100VG-AnyLAN physical frame structure is shown in figure 2-26. Each channel stream contains the:

- preamble (PRA)

- start frame delimiter (SFD)

- data sextets

- end frame delimiter

- filler bits

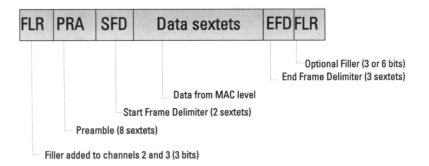

Figure 2-26

Filler Bits

A 3-bit filler is added to the preambles of channels 2 and 3. Additional fillers may be added to the EFD as needed to align the streams.

Preamble

The preamble for each channel stream is a sequence of eight sextets, as shown below.

010101 010101 010101 010101 010101 010101 010101 010101

Preambles are added to the beginning of each channel stream.

Start Frame Delimiter

The 2-sextet start frame delimiter is dependent on the priority of the packet. A high-priority packet SFD and normal-priority packet SFD are shown below.

High-Priority packet SFD:	**100000**	**111110**
Normal Priority packet SFD:	**111100**	**000011**

The same SFD is used for all channels.

End Sequence (End Frame Delimiter and Invalid Packet Marker)

The three-sextet end sequence is dependent on the error status of the packet. When a node transmits a packet, the End Frame Delimiter (EFD) is added to the end of the four data stream; if the hub detects an error in the packet as it is forwarding it, then an Invalid Packet Marker (IPM) is added to the end of all channel streams.

End Frame Delimiter   The end frame delimiter is one of two 3-sextet code combinations, depending on the original data patterns:

111111 000011 000001

000000 111100 111110

Invalid Packet Marker   An invalid packet marker (IPM) is used by the hub to mark an outgoing packet as "bad"—for example, a packet that was received containing transmission errors. The IPM bit sequence is shown below.

110000   011111   110000

Error Detection in 100VG-AnyLAN

The 100VG-AnyLAN 5B6B and channel offset scheme is designed to provide two types of error detection in conjunction with the use of the IEEE 802.3/802.5 standard CRC.

First, any three single bit errors in a packet will always be detected, that is, the code has a hamming distance of 4.

Second, by careful design of the code and by offsetting two of the channels relative to the other two channels, any error burst (that is, a pattern of errors occurring across the four wires) of duration 7 code bit periods is always detected. This means that burst error protection of 7 X 4 =28 code bits is provided.

Physical Medium Dependent (PMD) Sublayer

The Physical Medium Dependent (PMD) sublayer is the portion of the physical layer that defines link dependent processes. The PMD functions defined for 100VG-AnyLAN include:

- multiplexing for 2-pair and fiber-optic mediums

- NRZ coding

- providing media electrical and mechanical specifications

- link status control

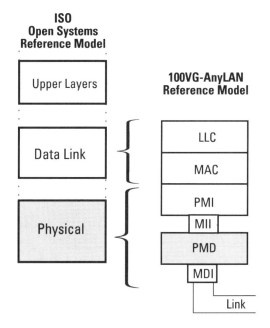

Figure 2-27

4-channel Multiplexing

The PMD sublayer is responsible for converting the 4-channel data streams into a format that is usable on non-4-pair mediums such as:

- two-pair, shielded twisted-pair

- fiber-optic cable

The PMI/MII each have four transmit and four receive channels. If the link is a 2-pair shielded twisted pair or a fiber-optic cable , the PMD sublayer multiplexes the 4-channel data into one transmit channel and one receive channel, as shown in figure 2-28 and figure 2-29, respectively. The receive and transmit channels each transmit at 120 MBaud per second (100 Mbit/sec NRZ = 120 MBaud/sec after 5B6B encoding).

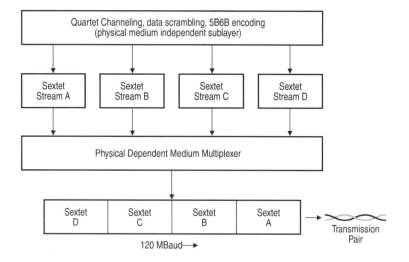

Figure 2-28

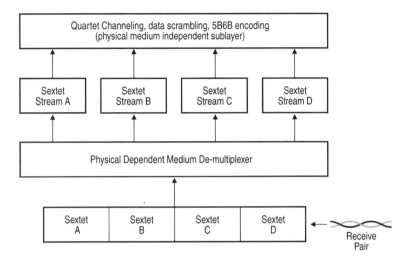

Figure 2-29

5B/6B Block Encoding with Non-Return to Zero (NRZ) Symbol Shaping

Non-return to Zero (NRZ) symbol shaping is a two-level, non-return-to-zero signaling mechanism used to transmit data and link-status control signals onto the physical medium. Using NRZ encoding, one bit of data is transmitted per clock cycle. A bit value of 1 is detected when a high voltage signal is transmitted, and a bit value of 0 is detected when a low voltage level signal is transmitted.

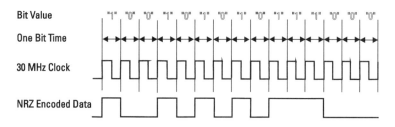

Figure 2-30

In addition to providing an efficient method for data transmission, quartet signaling with 5B/6B encoding allows 100VG-AnyLAN to operate on voice-grade, category 3 UTP cable. Using a 30-MHz clock, NRZ encoding generates a maximum, fundamental (non-harmonics) transmission frequency of 15 MHz on the cable medium—a transmission frequency of 15 MHz is derived from considering a worst-case data pattern of 10101010.... Before filtering, this data pattern would produce a 15-MHz square wave pattern.

This encoding allows the signal to be filtered before 30 MHz so as to prevent electromagnetic interference and pass US and International Regulatory requirements. It also keeps the signal within the useful operating range of cat 3 wire. Receive filters reject high frequency noise sources. This results in a robust signaling scheme which will perform well in 10Base-T environments.

4-UTP Link Medium Operation

To transmit 100 MBit/s signals over 4-pair, unshielded twisted-pair, the packet is first split into 5-bit data quintets. The quintets are scrambled, and then encoded into 6-bit sextets.

The PMD sublayer provides transmit and receive functions to control the link status and to facilitate message flow between the end node or a 100VG-AnyLAN hub and the physical medium. The PMD transmit functions include the transmission of both data and control signals. The link medium operation for a 4-UTP 100VG-AnyLAN network uses both full-duplex and half-duplex modes of operation, as shown in figure 2-31.

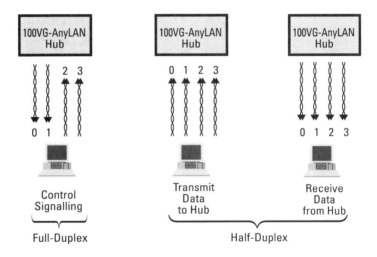

Figure 2-31

Note that controlling signals are transmitted with simultaneous, two-way control. The data transmissions are transmitted in half duplex—one transmission at a time. A 4-UTP 100VG-AnyLAN connection requires four twisted pairs for operation and uses the same pair configuration (1/2, 3/6, 4/5, and 7/8) as Ethernet and token ring, and as specified by the EIA/TIA 568 wiring standard.

Physical Layer (Layer 1)

Table 2-4 describes what twisted-pair wires are used for transmission by each channel.

Table 2-4

PMI Channel	Twisted-Pair Wires	EIA/TIA 568B Pair Assignment
0	1 and 2	2
1	3 and 6	3
2	4 and 5	1
3	7 and 8	4

Data Flow   After the data is NRZ encoded, the four sextets—one on each twisted-pair, are transmitted simultaneously. Transmission is continued, with four sextets transmitted simultaneously and in parallel, until the entire packet is transmitted.

The data is transmitted at 30 MBaud on each of the four link channels, using a 30 MHz clock. At the receiving end, the 30 MBaud of encoded data are received and decoded into 25 MBaud of the original data—resulting in an effective data rate of 100 Mbits per second (4 pairs times 25 Mbits per second per pair).

Link Status Control   Full duplex operation is required to communicate link-status control information between the hub and an end node. A combination of control tones transmitted on two of the pairs is used to communicate the link state between a hub and an end node or between cascaded repeaters. Channels 0 and 1 (twisted-pairs pairs 2 and 3) are used to communicate status between the hub to the end node; channels 2 and 3 (twisted-pairs 1 and 4) are used to communicate the link status between the end node and the hub. A combination of two low-frequency tones are generated by the PMD:

- **Tone 1** is a repeating pattern of sixteen consecutive 0s, followed by sixteen consecutive 1s. After NRZ encoding and transmission at 30 MBaud, the frequency of Tone 1 is approximately .937 MHz.

- **Tone 2** is a repeating pattern of eight consecutive 0s, followed by eight consecutive 1s. After NRZ encoding and transmission at 30 MBaud, the frequency of Tone 1 is approximately 1.875 MHz.

100VG-AnyLAN communicates status commands between the hub and the end node using a combination of these two tones. The meaning of the combinations of tones depend on whether they are transmitted by the end node, by a down-link port of a level 1 (root) hub, or by the up-link port of a level 2 hub, as shown in table 2-5 (transmitted control signal tones) and table 2-6 (received control signal tones).

Table 2-5

Tone Pair		Transmitted by end node	Transmitted by level 1 (root) hub	Transmitted by level 2 (cascaded) hub
Tone 1	Tone 1	Idle	Idle	Idle
Tone 1	Tone 2	Normal Priority Request	Incoming Data Packet	Normal Priority Request
Tone 2	Tone 1	High priority Request	Round-Robin Pre-empt	High priority Request
Tone 2	Tone 2	Link Training Request	Link Training Request	Link Training Request

Table 2-6

Tone Pair		Received by end node	Received by level 1 (root) hub	Received by level 2 (cascaded) hub
Tone 1	Tone 1	Idle	Idle	Idle
Tone 1	Tone 2	Incoming data packet	Normal Priority request	Incoming data packet
Tone 2	Tone 1	Reserved	High priority Request	Round-Robin Pre-empt
Tone 2	Tone 2	Link Training Request	Link Training Request	Link Training Request

Idle indicates that the round-robin cycle is complete and that no requests or packets are pending.

Normal Priority Request indicates that the end node is requesting to send a normal priority packet to the hub.

High Priority Request indicates that the end node is requesting to send a high- priority packet to the hub.

Incoming Data Packet indicates to an end node that a packet may be destined for that port. The end node is instructed to stop sending control tones on channels 2 and 3 in preparation for receipt of the packet.

Round Robin Pre-empt is the signal to lower level hubs that the lower-level hubs should not service another normal-priority request because another hub on the network is ready to service a high-priority request. After completing the current transmission, lower-level hubs relinquish transmission control until the high-priority transmission is complete.

If the current normal-priority round-robin cycle is not complete, the upper-level hub goes back to the pre-empted hub for completion of the round-robin cycle after all high-priority requests have been serviced. If the current round-robin is complete, the upper-level hub services the next port with a request pending (in port order).

Link Training Request initiates link training. Link training (training idle) is accomplished by sending a series of training packets in each direction between hub and end nodes.

2-STP and Fiber-Optic Link Medium Operation

The link medium operation for a 2-STP and a fiber-optic link are identical—both use one channel to transmit data and another channel to receive data. The link medium operation for a 2-STP and fiber-optic 100VG-AnyLAN network uses dual simplex control of operation, as shown in the STP example in figure 2-32.

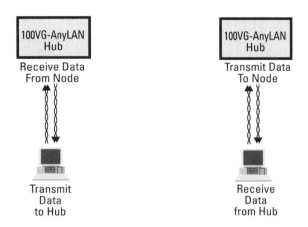

Figure 2-32

A 2-STP 100VG-AnyLAN connection requires two twisted pairs for operation (a twisted-pair for transmitting data and a twisted-pair for receiving data) and uses the same pair configuration as specified by the EIA/TIA 568 wiring standard.

A fiber-optic 100VG-AnyLAN connection requires two fibers—one fiber for transmitting data and one fiber for receiving data.

Data Flow on a Single-Level, 4-UTP Network

The MAC frame is decomposed, scrambled, and encoded at the source node before each transmission, and then decoded, unscrambled, recomposed and error-checked at the destination end node. If the source and destination end nodes are not attached to the same hub, the receive and retransmit process is performed at each intermediate hub.

Figure 2-33 is an example of the data flow between a source node (PC 1) and a destination node (PC 2) in a 100VG-AnyLAN single-hub 4 UTP network.

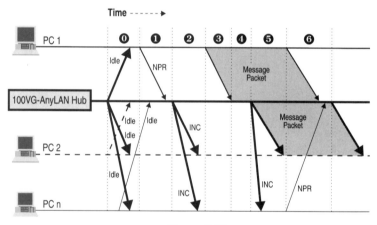

Figure 2-33

The network is idle at time= 0. In the idle state, the hub is sending out idle signals (tone 1 on channel 0 and tone 1 on channel 1 to all connected end nodes). The end nodes are also sending out idle signals (tone 1 on channel 2 and tone 1 on channel 3).

❶ The source node (PC 1) sends a normal-priority request (NPR) to the hub (tone 1 on channel 2 and tone 2 on channel 3) requesting to send a normal-priority packet on the network.

During its round-robin scan procedures, the hub selects the source end node and stops sending control tones (idles) to it. This will clear the link to allow the end node to transmit the packet on all four channels.

❷ The hub then alerts all potential destination nodes on the network segment that a packet may be destined for them by sending an Incoming (INC) message (tone 1 on channel 0 and tone 2 on channel 1).

The potential destination end nodes stop sending control tones on channel 2 and channel 3. This clears the link to allow the end node to receive the packet on all four channels.

Meanwhile PC 1 detects that its link is clear and forwards the message packet from the media access control sublayer to the physical medium independent sublayer in preparation for data transmission.

The physical medium independent sublayer in PC 1 separates the data into four channels, scrambles the five-bit quartets, and encodes the quintets into six-bit (5B6B) symbols. The preamble, start frame delimiter, and end frame delimiter are added to each channel. The frame is sent to the physical medium dependent sublayer.

❸ The physical medium dependent sublayer in PC 1 begins to send the packet to the hub using NRZ encoding.

❹ As the hub receives the packet, it decodes the destination address.

❺ The packet is routed to the end node(s) with the matching destination address—in this case, PC 2.

❻ At the same time, the hub stops sending INC and begins to send Idle (tone 1 on channel 0 and tone 1 on channel 1 1) to all other end nodes. All other end nodes resume sending requests (if they have something to send) or idles (if they have nothing to send).

Data Flow on a 4-UTP, Cascaded Network

Data flow in cascaded networks is similar to the data flow in a single-level network. The interconnected hubs act as a single large repeater. All traffic is sent to each hub, and each hub polls its active ports for requests after each packet transmission.

The level-1 (root) hub has primary control of the network.

The root hub begins servicing requests—in port order. If the next port to be serviced is connected to an end node, the request is processed in the same manner as described in a single-level network.

All hubs and other end nodes in the network are alerted of a possible incoming packet. The destination address is decoded first by the root hub, and then by all lower-level hubs. If the address matches an end node on a hub's configuration list, the packet is forwarded to that end node and to any promiscuous ports. The packet is always forwarded to all other hubs on the network.

If the next port on the root hub is connected to a lower-level hub, the lower-level hub takes control of packet arbitration, and sends all of its requests to the root hub for one complete round-robin cycle. Once the round-robin cycle is completed on the lower-level hub, packet arbitration control returns to the root hub. The root hub continues processing requests from its ports (in port order)—if a request is from a end node, the hub processes the end node's request; if the next port is another hub, the lower level hub completes its round robin cycle as described above.

Data Flow in a 2-STP or Fiber-Optic Network

Like the 4-UTP data flow described above, the flow of data between the source end node and the destination end node begins when the upper layer software on the source node advises its media access sublayer that it has a packet to send on the network. After receiving the packet, the MAC sublayer adds the source layer and any required pad bits to complete the data field.

In a 2-STP or fiber-optic 100VG-AnyLAN network, however, one shielded twisted-pair or fiber channel is used as a *dedicated* transmit channel; the other shielded twisted-pair (or other fiber channel) is used as a *dedicated* receive channel—Recall that in the 4 UTP 100VG-AnyLAN network, all four pairs of wires were required to send data or to receive data. The dual-simplex method utilized by STP and fiber optic 100VG-AnyLAN networks allows any PC to send a request on its transmit channel independent of receiving data on its receive line.

Figure 2-34 is an example of the data flow between a source node (PC 2) and a destination node (PC 1) in a 100VG-AnyLAN single-hub STP network.

Data Flow in a 2-STP or Fiber-Optic Network

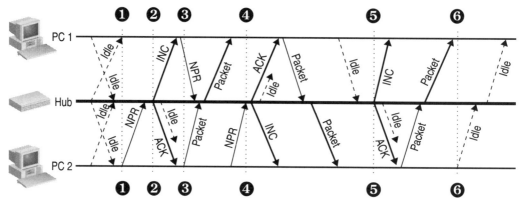

Figure 2-34

The network is idle at time= 0. In the idle state, the hub sends idle signals to all of its connected PCs. The end nodes are also sending out idle signals to the hub.

❶ The source node (PC 2) sends a normal-priority request (NPR) to the hub on its transmit circuit to the hub.

❷ The hub receives the normal-priority request on its receive circuit, and alerts all potential destination nodes on the network segment that a packet may be destined for them by sending an Incoming (INC) message on its transmit line. The hub also acknowledges the request from PC 2. Note that there is no need for any end node to clear its circuit (as in the 4 UTP), since each circuit is dedicated.

The physical medium independent sublayer in PC 2 separates the data into four channels, scrambles the five-bit quartets, and encodes the quintets into six-bit (5B6B) symbols. The preamble, start frame delimiter, and end frame delimiter are added to each channel. The frame is sent to the physical medium dependent sublayer, where it is multiplexed into one transmit channel. The physical medium dependent sublayer in PC 2 begins to send the packet to the hub using NRZ encoding.

❸ PC 2 receives the ACK on its receive circuit, and sends the packet to the hub. As the hub receives the packet, it decodes the destination address. Meanwhile, PC 1 wants to transmit, and sends a NPR to the hub. The hub buffers the request from PC 1, and proceeds to complete transmission of the original packet from PC 2 to the destination node (PC 2).

Since the transmit and receive circuits on PC 2 are independent, PC 2 sends another NPR—requesting to send anther packet. This request is also buffered.

❹ After sending the original packet, the hub:
   a. Goes through the round robin (on a port-order basis), looking for the next request. Since no pending request is high-priority, it looks for the next normal-priority request.
   b. Recognizes the NPR from PC 1 first (since PC 2 has just transmitted).
   c. Processes the NPR from PC 1.
   d. Sends the ACK to PC 1 (acknowledging the request) and sends INC to all other connected nodes on the network.

PC 1 sends the packet to the hub, and the hub completes transmission by decoding the destination address (in this case, PC 2) and sends the packet to PC 2.

Note that, once a transmission has been completed (a ACK, for example), it is immediately followed by an Idle signal. This again is possible because of the independent transmit and receive signals.

❺ The hub, when completed with its transmission, continues its round robin, recognizes that PC 2 has a pending request—and sends INC signals to all nodes except PC 2. The hub ACKs PC 2, and PC 2 transmits the packet.

❻ After completing all requests, the network returns to an idle state.

Cable Requirements on a 4-UTP 100VG-AnyLAN Network

The 100VG-AnyLAN network is designed to operate on the same 4-UTP cable and the same environment that is used in 10Base-T and token ring networks.

Cable Specifications

Several standards specify the requirements for the 4-pair, 100Ω cabling used in 100VG-AnyLAN. The EIA/TIA-568 standard, and associated System Bulletins, the EIA/TIA TDD-49, and the EIA/TIA-36, and the AT&T 258 Premises Distribution System specify the physical connection pin assignments, pair assignments, pair color coding, transmission characteristics, test parameters, test methods, and wiring practices for category 3, 4, and 5 four-pair, 100Ω, unshielded twisted-pair (UTP) cabling and associated hardware.

Twisted-pair cabling includes a variety of twisted-pair cable types with a nominal impedance of 100Ω. It comes in cables of four pairs or bundles of 25 or more pairs, and can be either shielded or unshielded. The cable used in a 100VG-AnyLAN network is the same cable used in 10 Mbit/second 10Base-T networks.

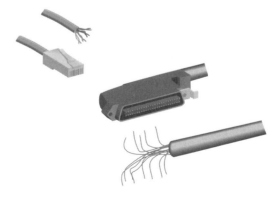

Figure 2-35

Twisted-pair cable is available in a variety of categories in both unshielded and shielded types:

Table 2-7

Category	Bandwidth	Designation	Pairs Required
Category 3	15 MHz	Voice grade	4 pairs
Category 4	20 MHz		4 pairs
Category 5	100 MHz	Data grade	2 or 4 pairs

Unshielded Category 3 cable is standard telephone cable. The connectors used in a 100VG-AnyLAN network are the same connectors used in telephone systems—RJ-45 (8-pin) or 50-pin telco connectors. In addition, standard telephone cross-connect blocks can be used for cable administration; adds, changes, and drops can be made in the same way as in the telephone system.

The proposed standard for 100VG-AnyLAN-style twisted-pair cable specifies that the cables be run in point-to-point cable segments. Each segment connects to network devices at each end of the cable. All cable sections must use twisted-pairs; *no flat wire is permitted anywhere on the network.* The nominal maximum length of a Category 3 cable segment is 100 meters—this includes all cabling in the path between two network devices.

If your cable is rated Category 3, then, in most cases, it will work at 100 meters, regardless of the manufacturer. Building wiring standards also specify Category 3 cable—supporting up to 100 meter cable lengths. Some sub-category 3 cables (for example, a cable that uses thinner gauge wire) may be used for 100VG-AnyLAN, but for shorter distances. Sub-category 3 cable must still meet the 100VG-AnyLAN cable specifications for 4-UTP cable. The tighter specifications of category 4 and 5 cables can support longer distances—for example, category 5 is supported at 150 meters.

Cabling may go through punch-down blocks or patch panels in a wiring closet and can connect to RJ-45 wall jacks in the work area or be terminated with RJ-45 plug connectors.

Figure 2-36 illustrates the EIA/TIA 568B pin assignments for an 8-pin RJ-45 plug, the color code identification, and the pair configuration for an 8-wire, 4-pair UTP cable. Note that although this references the EIA/TIA 568B pair and color code assignments, the EIA/TIA 568A standards may also be used as long as the cable is wired straight-through from the hub to the node, and remains twisted throughout its run.

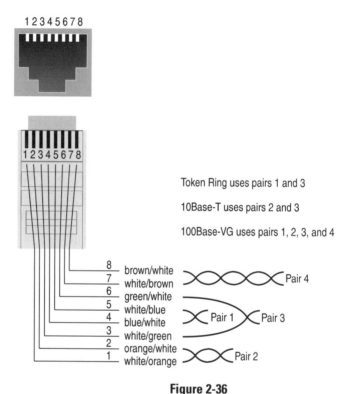

Figure 2-36

If you are currently running a token ring network using 4-pair UTP, you are probably using pairs 1 and 3; if you are currently running a 10Base-T network using 4-pair UTP, you are probably using pairs 2 and 3. *100VG-AnyLAN requires all 4 pairs* (pairs 1, 2, 3, and 4). Data transmission or data reception requires all four pairs at once—in one direction—either from the end node to the hub, or from the hub to the end node. The Demand Protocol access protocol requires the control signals from end node-to-hub to occur on pairs 1 and 4 and the control signals from hub-to-end-node to occur on pairs 2 and 3.

Testing 100VG-AnyLAN 4 UTP Cable

Table 2-8 summarizes the cable test parameters and their acceptable ranges for 100VG-AnyLAN operation. 100VG-AnyLAN has the same cable parameters as those requires for 10Base-T with the additional requirements of being able to test all four pairs, at test frequencies up to 15 MHz.

Table 2-8

Frequency	5 MHz	10 MHz	15 MHz
Maximum attenuation (dB/100m)	< 11.5 dB	< 11.5 dB	< 13.5 dB
Characteristic impedance (Ω)	85-115Ω	85-115Ω	85-115Ω
4 Pair, Pair-to-Pair Crosstalk (dB)	> 30.5 dB	> 26.0 dB	> 23 dB

Test Frequency

To verify the proper operation of the cable for 100VG-AnyLAN installation, the cable must be tested using signals in the 5 to 15 MHz frequency range.

Attenuation

Attenuation is the amount of signal strength or power that the electrical signal loses as a result of traveling over the wire. The longer the cable, the higher the attenuation. If the attenuation is too high, the receiver may not be able to reliably decode the data. The maximum total attenuation of a complete cable path between a 100VG-AnyLAN hub and an end node is 11.5 dB at 5 MHz and 10 MHz, and 13.5 dB at 15 MHz. This includes 1.5 dB due to reflections.

Characteristic Impedance

The magnitude of the differential characteristic impedance at all frequencies (between 1 and 15 MHz) must be between 85 and 115 Ω.

4-Pair Pair-to-Pair Crosstalk

Pair-to-pair crosstalk is the interference of a signal on one pair from another adjacent pair. The crosstalk attenuation between each wire pair and each other pair in the same cable pair bundle must be at least 30.5 dB at 5 MHz, 26.0 dB at 10 MHz, and 23 dB at 15 MHz.

Multiple Disturber Near-End Crosstalk (MDNEXT)

Multiple Disturber Near-End crosstalk (MDNEXT) measures the amount of signal interference from signals present on multiple wire pairs to a single wire pair—as measured at the near end, or closest to the generation point. If crosstalk interference at the near end is too high, it may cause interference with received signals. This is particularly important to measure on 25-pair binder groups, but is rarely an issue with 4-pair if the pair-to-pair specifications are met.

Verifying Cable for 100VG-AnyLAN Installations

When testing 100VG-AnyLAN cable, verify that these measurements fall within the specified 100VG-AnyLAN values for 100VG-AnyLAN cable characteristics:

- attenuation

- pair-to-pair crosstalk

- Multiple disturber near-end crosstalk

To correctly verify cable for 100VG-AnyLAN installations, all tests should be run—on all four pairs of the twisted-pair cable. Running a subset of the tests does not provide a complete test of the cable.

Cable testing must also be competed from end to end—from the end that attached to the hub to the end that attaches to the end node. *Testing portions of the cable is an incomplete test of the cable.* The pair-to-pair near -end crosstalk test must be completed from both ends of the cable. The remaining two tests may be completed from only one end of the cable.

Cable Test Devices

Several cable test devices are currently available that meet the specifications specified by the proposed 100VG-AnyLAN standard, and test on all four pairs of twisted-pair cable:

■ The HP J2263 Cable Test Set

■ The Microtest MT350 Scanner

■ The Fluke 652 Cable Meter

■ The Wavetek LANtech10

Each of the instruments are battery-operated and are available with an AC adapter. They all use RJ-45 connectors, and test all four pairs. Table 2-9 summarizes the measurement specifications for these instruments.

Table 2-9

LAN Tester	Signal Attenuation			Crosstalk Attenuation			Frequency Range
	Range	Resolution	Accuracy	Range	Resolution	Accuracy	
HP J2263 Cable Test Set	+1 to -50 dB	0.1 dB	± 2 dB at 100 ohms	+1 to -50 dB	0.1 dB	± 2 dB at 100 ohms	256, 512, 768 KHz, 1, 2, 4, 5, 8, 10, 16, 20 MHz
Microtest MT350 Scanner	+1 to -50 dB	0.1 dB	± 2 dB at 100 ohms	+1 to -50 dB	0.1 dB	± 2 dB at 100 ohms	256, 512, 768 KHz; 1, 2, 4, 5, 8, 10, 16, 20 MHz
Fluke 652 Cable Meter	+1 to -48 dB	0.1 dB	± 1 dB	+1 to -48 dB	0.1 dB	± 1 dB	5 to 10 MHz in 100 KHz steps; 10 to 20 MHz in 200 KHz steps
Wavetek LANtech10	0-40 dB	0.1 dB	±1 dB	0-36 dB	0.1 dB	±2 dB	5 MHz 10 MHz

Shielded Twisted-Pair (STP) Cable

Standards for 2-shielded twisted pair (STP) 150Ω cabling provide a very stable basis for 100VG-AnyLAN within the existing cable infrastructure. The EIA/TIA 568 standard, TSB-36 and 40, as well as the proposed new 568A standard presented via SB2840 specifies pin assignments, color coding, performance characteristics, and wiring strategy for this cabling system and associated hardware.

A 100VG-AnyLAN shielded twisted-pair link consists of the shielded twisted-pair- link medium, two end-connectors, and connection devices such as patch panels and wall plates.

This 2-pair STP cabling is traditionally supported by cables designated as types 1, 2, 6, and 9, and by extended specifications designated by an A-suffix, types 1A, 2A, 6A, and 9A providing for specified high frequency performance standards to 300 MHz. The type certification program is administered by Underwriters' Laboratories for any manufacturer wishing to gain certification of cabling products to these type designation. Table 2-10 describes these generic cable types and applications.

Table 2-10

Cable Type	Wiring Configuration	Wire Type	American Wire Gauge (AWG)	Typical usage
1	2 pairs shielded	solid	22	mainly data—work area to wiring closet (can be used outdoors)
2	2 pairs shielded 4 pairs unshielded	solid solid	22 22	voice and data—work area to wiring closet (can be used outdoors)
6	2 pairs shielded	stranded	26	patch panel or device to wall jack
9	2 pairs shielded	stranded or solid	26	Data—work areas to wiring closet (not outdoors, in conduit, or in closed raceways)

Type 1 or 2 cables, typically used in horizontal wiring for the wiring closet to the work area, allow 100m maximum lobe length. Standard patch panels can be used for cable management. As shown in figure 2-37, STP used for 100VG-AnyLAN usually terminates with a male DB-9 connector or data connector.

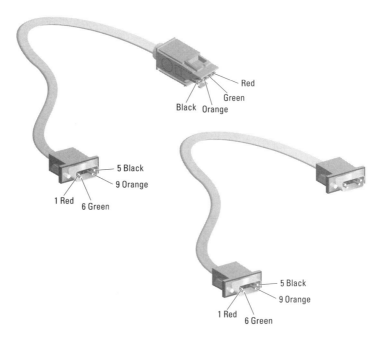

Figure 2-37

The color code and traditional token ring signal assignments are described in table 2-11.

Table 2-11

EIA/TIA conductor Identification	Color Code	Pin	From Node	From Hub
Pair 1	Red	1	RX +	TX +
	Green	6	RX -	TX -
Pair 2	Orange	9	TX -	RX -
	Black	5	TX +	RX +

Cabling may use existing patch panels in wiring closets, as well as using existing wall outlets in work areas.

As with traditional token ring function, both pairs are used in 100VG-AnyLAN.

Testing 100VG-AnyLAN STP Cable

Table 2-12 summarizes key test parameters for STP horizontal wiring using type 1A or 2A cable as specified in EIA/TIA SB-2840.

The cable should be tested at $25°$ C $\pm 3°$ C. 100VG-AnyLAN has the same type of parameters as those required for token ring.

Table 2-12

Frequency	10 MHz	30 MHz	60 MHz
Cable			
Maximum attenuation (dB/100m)	< 3.6 dB	< 6.8 dB	< 9.6 dB
Characteristic impedance (Ω)	$150 \pm 10\%$	$150 \pm 10\%$	$150 \pm 10\%$
Near-end crosstalk (dB)	>53.5 dB	>46.3 dB	>41.8
Data Connector			
Near End Crosstalk (dB)	> 65	>56.9	>50.9
Maximum insertion loss (dB)	0.10	0.15	0.20

Such installations are generally not tested for certification. Rather, the cable components are certified, and installation guidelines are designed to ensure appropriate performance. If testing is desirable to verify performance parameters, there are a numbers of test tools available to simplify this task:

- Scope Communications Inc. Wiretest 16

- Wavetek Corporation LANTech 10 and LANTech 100

- HP J2263A Cable Test Set

Fiber-Optic Cable

The proposed 100VG-AnyLAN standard supports the fiber-optic standards described in the EIA/TIA-568 standard SC connectors. Patch cables to existing ST and SMA are readily available.

A 100VG-AnyLAN fiber-optic link consists of the fiber-optic link medium, two end-connectors and connection devices such as patch panels and wall plates.

Fiber-Optic Link Medium is made up of a minimum of two strands of optical fiber, running parallel to each other, enclosed in a protective jacket. Each optical fiber is usually composed of glass, with a nominal 62.5/125 µm core/cladding diameter. If you purchase dual-window fiber-optic cable, you can use it at both 850-nm and 1330 nm wavelengths.

Each 62.5/125 µm fiber should meet the specifications described in table 2-13.

Table 2-13

Parameter	850 nm	1300 nm
Attenuation	3.75 dB/km	1.5 dB/km
Modal and width	160 MHz-km	500 MHz-km
Dispersion Slope		0.093 ps/km-nm^2
Dispersion Minimum		1365 nm

100VG-AnyLAN Network Topology Rules

The topology rules and recommendations for 100VG-AnyLAN networks may look familiar to you since 100VG-AnyLAN technology uses the network design rules and topologies of 10Base-T and token-ring networks. The topology rules for Ethernet and token ring will work for 100VG-AnyLAN.

This section includes some 100VG-AnyLAN design rules and recommendations. A note before you continue—a design rule is defined as "your network will not work unless you adhere to this"; a recommendation is defined as "it will work, but it may affect your network performance or supportability of the network".

Rule: Your network topology must be in a physical star topology, with no branches, or loops.

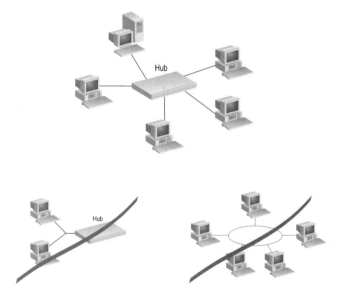

Figure 2-38

Rule: All four pairs are required in a 4-pair UTP network. If you are using 4-pair UTP twisted-pair wiring, do not split the pairs anywhere in the network. If you are upgrading your Ethernet 10Base-T or UTP token ring network to 100VG-AnyLAN, verify that all four pairs are available throughout the network. 10Base-T networks require only two twisted pairs—and the other two pairs may often be routed at cross-connect (punch-down) blocks, to the telephone network or left unconnected.

Rule: Do not use flat cable in a twisted-pair topology. When using twisted-pair wiring, be sure to keep the pairs twisted all the way up to the pins of the cross-connect blocks. Unintentional miswiring often occurs at cross connect blocks (punch-down blocks) and patch panels. A section of flat, untwisted wire can cause crosstalk, especially at the cross connect blocks.

Rule: There may be only one active path between any two hubs in the network.

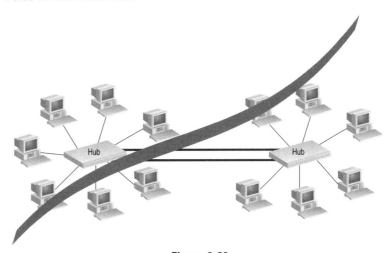

Figure 2-39

It is permissible, however, to have multiple paths between two 100VG-AnyLAN hubs, bridges, or routers *as long as only one is active at any one time.*

By designing redundant, backup connections into your network, you ensure that a hardware or cable failure on the primary network component will not affect the ability to communicate between nodes.

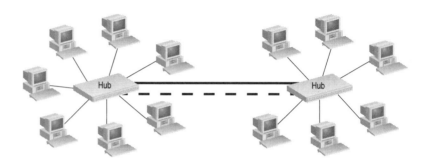

Figure 2-40

Though the proposed 100VG-AnyLAN specifications address redundant links on a hub, your hardware may not support redundant, back-up links.

Rule: No more than 1024 nodes are allowed on a single-shared (unbridged) 100VG-AnyLAN.
You should try to limit your singled-shared (single 100 Mbit/sec domain) 100VG-AnyLAN to under 250 nodes. Unlike Ethernet, where the node limitation is dependent on collision detection, this recommendation is based on network performance. The actual maximum nodes allowed on a 100VG-AnyLAN single-shared network is 1024, though you may experience network degradation at 250 or more nodes. You will probably not find the 250-node count very limiting since several, smaller sub-networks joined by bridges or routers are easier to manage, easier to troubleshoot, and usually provide better network performance than one large, single-shared network.

Recommendation: You should have less than 2.5 kilometers between any two nodes on a single-shared (single 100 Mbit/sec domain) 100VG-AnyLAN network.

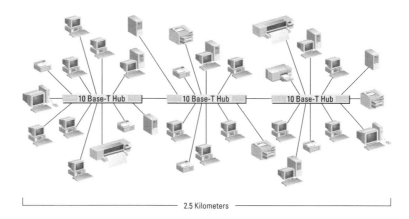

Figure 2-41

Rule: All nodes in a single-shared (single 100 Mbit/sec domain) 100VG-AnyLAN network must use the same 100VG-AnyLAN-supported packet format (IEEE 802.3 Ethernet or IEEE 802.5 token ring format). Multiple packet formats are not supported on a single-shared (single 100 Mbit/sec domain) 100VG-AnyLAN network. If you want to connect an token-ring-frame-format-based network to a Ethernet-frame-format-based network, you must use a token-ring-to-Ethernet 100VG-AnyLAN bridge.

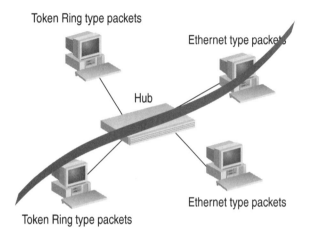

Figure 2-42

Note that if you want to connect an IEEE 802.5-frame-format-based 100VG-AnyLAN LAN to a 4 Mbit/second or 16 Mbit/second token ring network, only a 4-to-100 or 16-to-100 speed-conversion bridge is necessary. The 100VG-AnyLAN token ring frame is fully compatible with the 4 Mbit/second or 16 Mbit/second token ring frame.

If you want to connect an Ethernet-frame-format-based 100VG-AnyLAN LAN to an 10 Mbit/sec Ethernet network, only a 10-to-100 speed-conversion bridge is necessary. The 100VG-AnyLAN Ethernet frame is fully compatible with the 10 Mbit Ethernet frame.

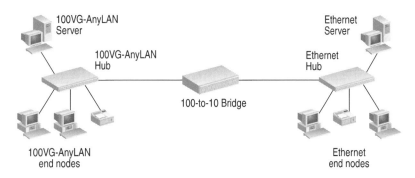

Figure 2-43

Recommendation: Minimize the levels of cascading. Your network will perform best if you keep it under three levels of hub cascading, thus minimizing arbitration overhead.

Rule: Between any two nodes in a network, you should have no more than 7 bridges. This is a IEEE 802.1D Spanning Tree protocol recommendation, and is a useful limit for non-spanning-tree networks as well.

Designing 100VG-AnyLAN Networks

A review of 100VG-AnyLAN basic physical connections may be necessary before designing your 100VG-AnyLAN network. Understanding these connections will aid you in making your designs.

Cables

In a typical 100VG-AnyLAN installation, the 100VG-AnyLAN hub will probably be installed in a wiring closet, or on a desktop with one cable directly connecting a port on the 100VG-AnyLAN hub and an end node.

If your hub is installed in a wiring closet, cable can be installed in floors, walls, or ceilings. More than likely, your cable installation will already support 100VG-AnyLAN upgrades. When installing cable, be sure to adhere to your building codes. For example,when installing cable in air ducts, air plenums, and other environmental air spaces, most building codes require fire-rated cable. Your building code may impose other, specific restrictions on cable types.

These types of cables are commonly used in an 100VG-AnyLAN network:

- 4-pair unshielded, voice-grade twisted-pair with an RJ-45 connector on each end of the cable (Cat 3, 4, 5)

- 2-pair shielded twisted-pair with DB-9 connectors

- 25-pair unshielded twisted pair cable using 50-pin telco connector at each end of the cable for use in cross connect blocks

- A fiber-optic cable

Figure 2-44

Computers

To connect a computer to the network, the computer must have a 100VG-AnyLAN network interface card (NIC), also called a LAN adapter. This card plugs into the computer's I/O bus and attaches to the 100VG-AnyLAN network.

The RJ-45 connector of an unshielded twisted-pair cable just plugs into the RJ-45 receptacle until the tab of the connector clicks into place.

The DB-9 STP connector of a shielded twisted-pair cable slides onto the receptacle.

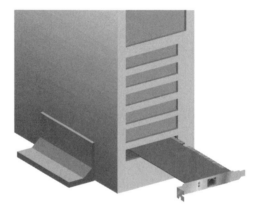

Figure 2-45

Hubs

100VG-AnyLAN hubs may have homogeneous connectors or a variety of connectors — RJ-45 ports for connection to twisted-pair cable, and fiber-optic connectors for connection to fiber-optic cables. A hub may also have a special uplink port for connection to another 100VG-AnyLAN hub.

Cross-Connect Blocks

Cross-connect blocks, often referred to as punch-down blocks, allow easy management of twisted-pair wiring. Cross-connect blocks use patch cables to connect signal sources to appropriate destinations. Using cross-connect blocks, it is easy to manage the adds, moves and drops that are typical of a network.

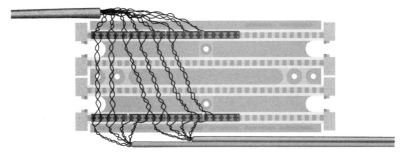

Figure 2-46

Note that the proposed 100VG-AnyLAN standard requires that there be no flat wire in a twisted-pair cable segment; it must all be twisted. This is particularly important when dealing with cross-connect blocks—it is easy for crosstalk to occur in the presence of so many signals in a small area. Make extra sure that all pairs remain twisted all the way up to the pins of the blocks.

A Single Hub 100VG-AnyLAN Network

Building a network with a single 100VG-AnyLAN hub is simple—just connect the cable (twisted-pair cable for a twisted-pair 100VG-AnyLAN hub or fiber-optic cable for a fiber-optic 100VG-AnyLAN hub) between the nodes (computers, server, printer) and the hub, and you are ready to go.

The single, 100VG-AnyLAN hub forms a star configuration with its nodes, as shown in figure 2-47 below.

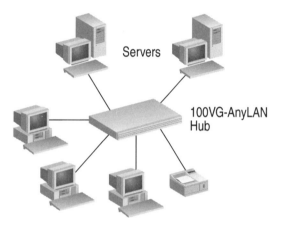

Figure 2-47

The implementation of this simple network—that is, the actual physical connections, can take a number of different forms.

Direct Wiring

Direct wiring, using twisted-pair or fiber-optic cable to connect the hub directly to the computers and server, is easy to install. The hub and cables are out in the open, where it is easily accessible to everyone. Moving or adding users can be cumbersome, however, since all of the cable — from desktop to hub—must be reinstalled or added. It can also be intrusive to troubleshoot the network, since the cable infrastructure and the users share the same space.

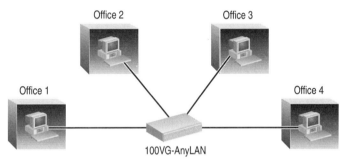

Figure 2-48

Wiring Closet

In most cases it is best to put the hub in a secure place. A wiring closet is ideal for this purpose. Cables can run from there to the work area in floors, walls, or ceilings. The cables can come out in wall plates, as shown in the figure below—note that the connection from the wall plate to the computer can be made with a short length of twisted-pair or fiber-optic cable.

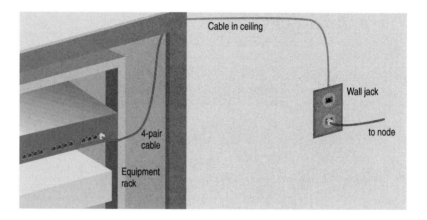

Figure 2-49

Placing the hub in the wiring closet also gives you the opportunity to centralize the wiring in your building.

You can use cross-connect blocks to route your LAN wiring via 4-pair cables to individual computers. You can also run several nodes' worth of wiring in a 25-pair bundle, and break it out into 4-pair cabling in a work area using a "harmonica"; this works well in open office situations. Such an arrangement is illustrated in the figure below. Note that you must keep the 4-pairs together—do not split the pairs when connecting to the cross-connect blocks.

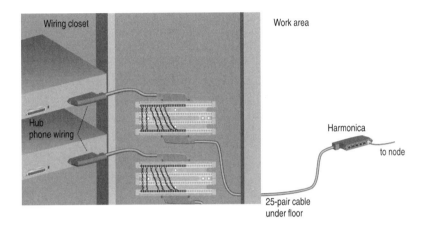

Figure 2-50

Multiple 100VG-AnyLAN Hub Networks

As your network grows, you may run out of hub ports. Instead of replacing your existing 100VG-AnyLAN hub, just add another hub to your network and connect them together.

Hubs in a Single Location

If your work group is located in one place, you will probably also want to keep your hubs in one place. You can connect additional hubs to the original hub using lengths of twisted-pair or fiber-optic cable (depending on your hub type). You must, however, use the up-link port on the lower-level hub when connecting it to an upper level hub, as shown below.

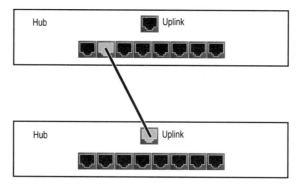

Figure 2-51

As in 10Base-T networks, when you cascade hubs, try to minimize the levels of cascading. Look at the network shown below.

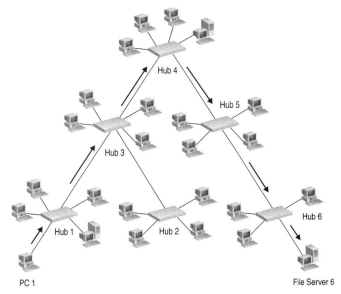

Figure 2-52

In this figure, there are three levels of hubs—a root hub (hub 4) and two lower layers of hubs. If PC 1 copies a file to file server 6:

1. PC 1 sends a request signal to Hub 1.

2. Hub 1 receives the request, and sends a request to hub 3.

3. Hub 3 receives the request, and sends a request to hub 4 (the root hub).

4. Hub 4 acknowledges the request to Hub 3

5. Hub 3 sends an acknowledgment to Hub 1.

6. The packet is sent through Hub 1, Hub 3, Hub 4, Hub 5, Hub 6, and then to file server 6.

If you minimize the levels of cascading—in this case, eliminating one level of cascading—you have minimized the round-trip delay of the arbitration signals, as shown below.

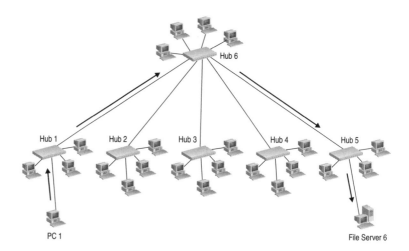

Figure 2-53

Distributed Hubs

When your hubs are distributed across your network, other factors—such as number of hubs in each location, and the distance between each location, affect your network design.

When you connect a hub in one location to another hub in another location, you can use the network medium (twisted-pair cable for twisted-pair hubs and fiber-optic for fiber-optic hubs) and the uplink port on the lower level hub. If you are using twisted-pair cable, be aware that the cable distance between Hub 1 and Hub 2 should not exceed the maximum length allowed by the cable specification. Overall, the distance between one end node and another end node should be less than 2.5 kilometers.

Sample Design Upgrades

The sample design upgrades used in the remaining part of this chapter are design upgrades based on the sample topologies introduced in Chapter 1. The sample networks will be updated, as appropriate, with 100VG-AnyLAN networking components.

Updating the Engineering Department with 100VG-AnyLAN

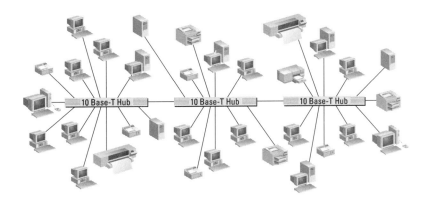

Figure 2-54

Suppose you were hired to design an network upgrade to the engineering department described in Chapter 1 (shown again in the figure above). You've done your homework—you've analyzed the engineering department and you have found the following:

■ The members of the clerical staff remark that the network seems to work the best in the early mornings. During that time, file transfers complete in a timely manner. After about 9:00 AM, however, the network response time varies from slow to s-l-o-w, and doesn't pick up until the next morning. The network performance *really* degrades after 2:00 PM. To be more productive, many of the accounting clerks and administrative assistants come to work early, take a short, early lunch, and leave work when the network is at its slowest. They try not to access the network during the slow times. Your network management software seems to confirm this—network performance of the LAN exceeds 18% during the mid-to-late afternoon hours, and collision rate is a high 8% during that time.

- In the last six months, 20 new engineers were hired. Many of the senior engineers have recently upgraded their workstations. They mention that the new workstations seem to have compounded the network performance problem—Their machines can go incredibly fast, but the network can't keep up. One engineer paraphrased the problem as "I replaced my horse and buggy with a Ferrari, but I feel like I'm still driving on unpaved roads".

- As with many of today's network, this network began as many fragmented, separate LANs. Very little planning was done when the workgroups were combined into one department LAN. The clerical staff and the engineering staff all share a single collision domain.

- The engineers use the network often to access CAD and simulation software, to transfer files from one workstation to another, and to print circuit designs. The files that are transferred and printed are typically very large.
The clerical staff primarily access two data base servers, and also utilizes the two network printers for company correspondence.

- The data collected by the network management software package noted that the busy time of day for the data base servers is the early morning and the busy time for the engineering servers was in midmorning and midafternoon —which also matches the clerical staff's observations. You also noticed that engineers in this company seem to prefer coming to work later than the clerical staff and left later in the day.

- The long-term network upgrade strategy is high speed networking, but the company can't afford to replace the category three unshielded twisted-pair wiring that was strung in the building five years ago.

The Upgrade Recommendation

Phase 1: Put the engineering staff on a high speed 100VG-AnyLAN segment immediately, and, for now, keep the clerical staff on the 10Base-T segment.

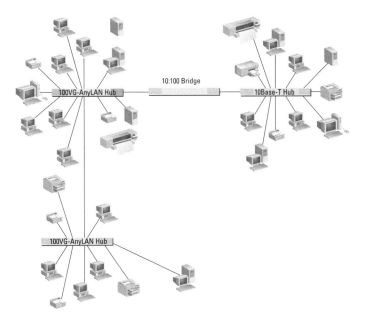

Figure 2-55

Reasoning Behind the Recommendation

- **Engineers need more bandwidth.** The engineering department has outgrown its 10 Mbit/sec network. The engineer's work is very network intensive and the 100 Mbit/sec speeds will relieve network congestion. Large, single burst activity like file transfers will not cause a bottleneck in the 100VG-AnyLAN high network speed as it currently does in the 10 Mbit/sec LAN.

- **Relieves congestion on the remaining 10 Mbit network**. The clerical staff also benefits with the upgrade since a major contributor to network congestion (bandwidth-hungry engineers) have been removed from their segment. The clerical staff should see a big improvement to overall network performance since the engineering traffic will be filtered—engineering network traffic will not affect the traffic on the clerical segment.

- **No need to update cable infrastructure.** A deciding factor for 100VG-AnyLAN was the cable infrastructure. Since the existing cable is 10Base-T compliant, it will work for 100VG-AnyLAN. High speed alternatives—FDDI and other fast copper-based networks, for example, require a major upgrade to the cable infrastructure—at a cost that is prohibitive to this company.

- **Upgrade will not greatly impact users.** Because the existing 10Base-T topology rules remain the same for 100VG-AnyLAN, the update is as easy as replacing a NIC in each end node, swapping the 10Base-T hub with a 100VG-AnyLAN hub, and plugging in cables.

With the addition of a simple, speed-matching bridge, engineers and clerical staff can communicate with each other without affecting each other's network.

Phase 2: In the future, upgrade the clerical staff to 100VG-AnyLAN

The Phase 1 upgrade will also alleviate the network congestion experienced by the clerical staff. The clerical network, however, is beginning to show signs of stress. The network administer should keep a close eye on this segment. Network performance metrics, like peak and average utilization, should be tracked.

Updating the Insurance Company with 100VG-AnyLAN

Your next consulting job is with a large insurance company, as described in Chapter 1,and reillustrated in the figure below. The network consists of two 16 Mbit/sec token ring, and a 4 Mbit/sec token ring.

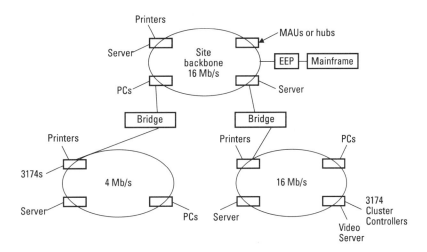

Figure 2-56

The claims adjusters, insurance agents, and accounting staff in this office rely heavily on their network. All financial accounting is done on site—with a mainframe located on the backbone. Reports are completed on a daily basis—with financial summaries due at corporate headquarters on a weekly and month basis. At year-end, a detailed financial report is completed.

The multi-media application began as an experiment here— and has been a resounding success. When a customer claim is received, it is immediately matched with its multi-media folder. The folder contains scanned pictures of a client's insured property, and voice annotations remarking on the value and condition of each piece is included in the folder.

A multi-media folder is opened for every new client. The folders are continuously kept up-to-date by the insurance agent.

Currently, an agent must walk over to one of three centrally located multi-media workstations to access the multi-media server.

The long term plan in this office is to replace paper files with multi-media folders, including multi-media accounting reports. By year end, the goal is to have 75 % of its claims adjusters and insurance agents on line in multi-media. Another multi-media server is in the budget for this year.

The Upgrade Recommendation

You recommend a phased upgrade.

Phase 1: Replace the video server token ring subnetwork with 100VG-AnyLAN, move the cluster controller to the backbone, and replace the 16 Mbit/sec bridge with a 16:100 speed matching bridge.

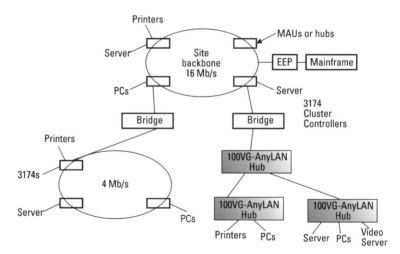

Figure 2-57

Reasoning Behind the Recommendation

- **Multi-media users need more bandwidth than currently available**. The original 16 Mbit/sec network was not intended to support multi-media to the desktop. Multi-media can generate a lot of network traffic, and a bigger pipe is needed to relieve network congestion.

- **The desktops are currently wired with STP cable**. If your current wiring infrastructure adheres to the IEEE 802.5 token ring wiring recommendations, you can be assured that it will work for 100VG-AnyLAN networks. The proposed 100VG-AnyLAN standard was built around existing IEEE 802.5 token ring (and IEEE 802.3 Ethernet) cabling standards.

- **The control of the network must be deterministic.** Multi-media packets are time sensitive. Some other copper-based high speed networks are probabilistic—they cannot guarantee access to the network. 100VG-AnyLAN networks and multi-media are a great combination—with 100VG-AnyLAN's high priority and normal-priority demand priority protocol and high speed, you can be assured that time-sensitive packets will be processed immediately.

- **Upgrading the network is simple.** Just replace the NIC in each PC and swap the network attachment unit with a 100VG-AnyLAN hub, and your 100VG-AnyLAN network is installed.

Phase 2: In the future, upgrade the 4 Mbit/sec token ring with 16 Mbit/sec token ring.

16 Mbit/sec token ring networks move data 4 times as fast as 4 Mbit/sec—use the equipment, if necessary, from the old 16 bit/sec token ring network.

100VG-AnyLAN Installation Check List

To upgrade to a 100VG-AnyLAN network, complete the following check list:

☐ Verify that the cable infrastructure meets 100VG-AnyLAN specifications. If the existing cabling infrastructure meets the IEEE 10Base-T or IEEE 802.5 token ring specifications, then it will work for 100VG-AnyLAN. Be sure to verify that all four pairs of the cat 3 UTP cable are available for use by the 100VG-AnyLAN network.

☐ Order a Network Interface Card (NIC) for each end node on the 100VG-AnyLAN network

☐ Order the 100VG-AnyLAN hub(s). If more than one hub is necessary to accommodate the number of end nodes, be sure to purchase hubs with built-in uplink ports. You will be able to easily cascade the 100VG-AnyLAN hubs with the uplink port.

☐ Schedule (and verify) upgrade date with your users

☐ Replace the Hub(s) or other network connection devices with the 100VG-AnyLAN hub(s) and power on the 100VG-AnyLAN hub.

☐ Replace the NIC with a 100VG-AnyLAN NIC

    ☐ Remove the network cable from the NIC

    ☐ Remove the NIC from the workstation, PC, or printer

    ☐ Install the 100VG-AnyLAN NIC in the workstation, PC, or printer. The NIC should be network ready—no configuration should be necessary

    ☐ Attach the cable to the 100VG-AnyLAN NIC

☐ Power on the workstation—the NIC will automatically communicate with the hub to verify cable and NIC functionality

3

Cross-Point Switching Technology and Network Design

Cross-point switching enhances 100VG-AnyLAN and Ethernet networks by providing simultaneous communication between segments. Like adding extra lanes on a highway to relieve traffic congestion, cross-point switches allow efficient use of the network by creating multiple data paths, in parallel. More users can access the network at the same time—minimizing congestion.

Cross-point switching in a 100VG-AnyLAN network works exactly the same way as cross-point switching in an Ethernet environment. The examples in this chapter assume an Ethernet since Ethernet cross-point switching equipment is currently readily available.

Ethernet Cross-Point Switching

Ethernet networks are based on a single-segment (collision domain) topology where access to the bus is provided to only one user at a time. As the network grows, and more users and servers are added to the network, network performance may begin to suffer because of network congestion. This type of network congestion is a common cause of poor performance on many of today's Ethernet networks. Ethernet cross-point switching can often be a performance booster because it allows packets to travel simultaneously, in parallel, among Ethernet segments.

Ethernet Cross-Point Switching

Ethernet cross-point switching technology is designed to ease traffic bottlenecks. By combining fast transmission speeds and circuit-switching technology, cross-point switching creates multiple data paths in parallel— supporting simultaneous conversations.

Compare this concept to a telephone switching system, figure 3-1.

Figure 3-1

Telephone switching systems support many simultaneous telephone conversations, without interruption to each other. The call between Frank and Sharon, for example, does not affect the call between Janis and Bob.

The route between two users may also change on a call-by-call basis. For example, the physical connection between Janis and Bob on Monday may not be the same line used to connect the two on Tuesday. Note that Janis is not aware of the physical connection made by the telephone switch—her only concern is getting a clear line to Bob, whatever that line is. The concept of Ethernet cross-point switching is similar to telephone switching.

Traditional Ethernet (Ethernet without switching) is a half-duplex technology based on a separate transmit (Tx) circuit and the receive (Rx) circuit. Only one circuit is active at a time. If both circuits are active, a collision is detected. When this occurs, the colliding nodes back off, and then attempt to retransmit their packets, after a random interval of time.

Ethernet Cross-Point Switching

The switching environment is analogous to a point-to-point connection. Switched, "point-to-point" connections between Ethernet LAN segments last only for the duration of the packet. New connections are made "on- the- fly" as shown in figure 3-2. As in the telephone analogy, users should not be aware of what physical circuit is used within the switch.

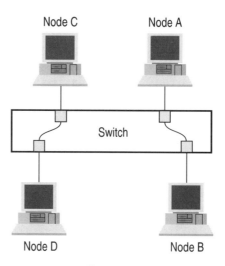

Figure 3-2

If Node A is transmitting a packet to Node B, the Ethernet cross-point switch connects only the lines from LAN segment A and LAN segment B since there is no need to send packets to any other ports. At the same time, node C wants to send a packet to node D. The Ethernet cross-point switch, using a different circuit, connects nodes C and D. Both circuits work in parallel—the two connected pairs are connected to two different LAN segments, each consisting of the two circuits in the Ethernet cross-point switch. The effective throughput of your Ethernet network, with the use of the Ethernet cross-point switch, has gone from 10 Mbits per second to 20 Mbits per second for the duration of the packet transmission. The increase in throughput is dependent on the number of LAN segments you can create with the LAN switch; the more ports on your switch, the higher the potential throughput of your Ethernet LAN—up to $\dfrac{number-of-ports}{2}$ times the bandwidth of your original network(each connection requires 2 ports on the switch). For example, a 10-port 10 MBit per second Ethernet LAN switch has the potential of providing up to 50 MBit per second throughput during the transmission of the five packets.

It is important to note that your network design and network protocol play an important part in determining the effectiveness of a cross-point switch. The performance of a peer-to-peer network can be greatly enhanced if you design the "point-to-point" connections to take advantage of multiple peer-to-peer conversations. A cross-point switch in a client-server environment is ineffective if the clients are distributed across the segments of the switch, all trying to access a server, thus prohibiting multiple conversations.

The Ethernet cross-point switch operates as a media access control (MAC)-layer device that is protocol independent—therefore the switch will not affect your use of IPX, TCP/IP and all other network-layer protocols.

Typical Ethernet Switching

A typical Ethernet cross-point switch consists of processors that act like miniature two-port bridges. One processor is associated with each port on the switch. The processors filter and forward packets based on the content of an internal address table and the contents of the packet. As with bridges, the address table is maintained and managed based on an aging interval. When a processor receives a packet it does not recognize, it "learns" the location of the new source and sends the packet to all of its output ports if the destination is unknown. When the response packet comes back, the address module learns its location and sets up the address table in all of the processors in the switch. Once the address table entry is made, subsequent packets are directly switched by the processor.

Typical Ethernet Switching Performance

Two key performance characteristics distinguish typical Ethernet cross-point switching from bridges and routers:

- Potential for low latency
- High Filtering and Forwarding Capability

Low Latency

Latency, or delay time, determines how long it takes a packet to enter the input port and begin to appear at the output port. As the cross-point switch begins to read a packet, the first six octets it encounters is the destination address. While the packet is still being received, the cross-point switch circuitry looks at its address table, and determines the correct destination. Packet destination decoding occurs while the packet is still arriving at the input LAN port. If the packet needs to be switched to another LAN segment and the destination LAN segment is not busy, the packet is immediately sent to the output port while it is still being received at the input port. If the destination segment is busy, the packet is buffered and sent as soon as the destination segment becomes available. Broadcast packets are synchronously transmitted to all output ports. The result is a latency time as low as 40 microseconds—regardless of packet size. Bridges and routers, in contrast, use store-and-forward technology, resulting in latency times dependent on packet size. By minimizing latency, packets move freely on the network, without degrading performance.

High Filtering and Forwarding Capability

The switching processors independently filter and forward all Ethernet packets at media speed. Each processor can switch an infinite stream of back-to-back packets without losing a packet, regardless of packet size. To help balance throughput when networks are operating at near peak, the processors also provide buffering. If the destination segment is busy, the packet is buffered and sent as soon as the destination segment becomes available—usually on a FIFO (first in, first out) basis.

Designing Ethernet Cross-Point Switched Networks

In a typical Ethernet network, file servers are located on the same segment as its clients. This eliminates costly interconnect time delays. Network managers must keep up with traffic patterns to ensure that packets travel in the most efficient way—when traffic patterns change, the network topology may also require changing.

Figure 3-3 represents a typical Ethernet, non-switched network.

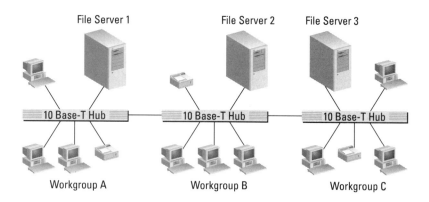

Figure 3-3

This 10-Base-T workgroup network consists of three 10Base-T hubs, three file servers, and many users. On a typical day, users in workgroup A access file server 1, users in workgroup B access file server 2, and users in workgroup C access file server 3. At month end, all servers must be accessible to all users. The department managers of Workgroup A, workgroup B and workgroup C must be able to access all three servers daily.

Since all the workgroups are in a single collision domain, when one user accesses the network, no other user can. For example, when a user in workgroup A retrieves a file from file server A, no other user in workgroup A, workgroup B, and workgroup C can use the network.

The network is starting to experience performance degradation—especially during peak times. The network manager has decided to install an Ethernet cross-point switch to this network. Before installing the switch, the network manager should:

- Monitor all segments of the network to verify the characteristics of its users—for example, the network manager should determine which users access which servers and printers.

- Segment the network and place local resources on segments with associated end nodes.

- Place global resources on their own segment

The network manager purchased an Ethernet cross-point switch, and implemented the following network:

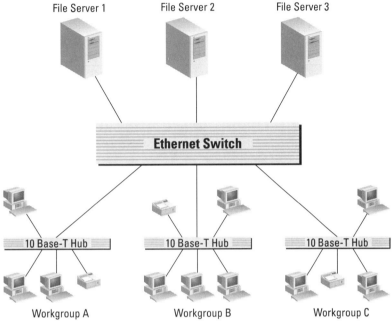

Figure 3-4

The network manager decided to:

- Group the end users into three separate segments—workgroup A, workgroup B, and workgroup C—very similar to what the network manager originally had implemented on the non-switched Ethernet network. Each segment attaches to a port of the switch.

- Since the servers were global resources—accessed by everyone on the network—the network manager decided to place each server on its own port of the switch.

- Keep the printers local to the workgroup because the printers are local resources, only used by the users in a specific workgroup.

Designing Ethernet Cross-Point Switched Networks

Three simultaneous conversations can now occur (users from
workgroup A communicating with File Server 1, users from
workgroup B communicating with File Server 2, and users from
workgroup C communicating with File Server 3) , boosting the peak
throughput of the network to 30 Mbit/sec. Since this is the normal
operation of the network, the switch has significantly increased
network performance.

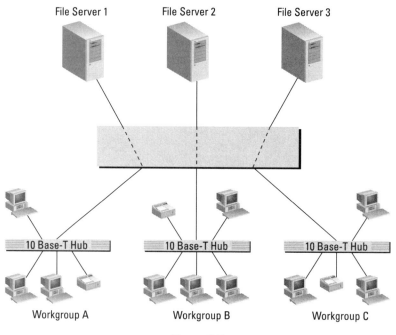

Figure 3-5

When NOT to Add Ethernet Switching

Ethernet cross-point switching technology was developed to enhance the throughput of local Ethernet networks. It was not meant to:

- Replace routers. An Ethernet cross-point switch does not provide connection to multiple protocol networks, or provide security firewalls.

- Ease traffic destined to a single resource. An Ethernet cross-point switch does not improve networks where there is heavy traffic destined to a single resource—For example, if most of your users access a single server, a switch will not boost performance.

Updating the Engineering Department With Ethernet Cross-Point Switching

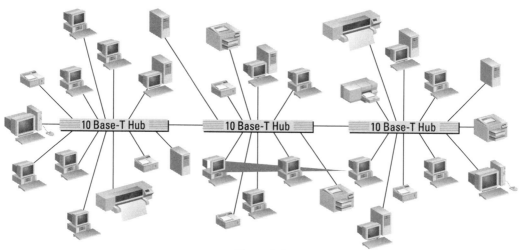

Figure 3-6

Suppose your Ethernet Engineering department network is having performance problems. Symptoms include:

- Variable (and sometimes poor) network response times.

- Extremely high peak utilization and very high average utilization statistics

- Unhappy users

Your current network is a single segment, single-collision-domain network. When you analyze the traffic pattern of your network, you notice clusters of activity. The clerical staff, for the most part, only access the clerical servers; the software engineers access the software servers, and the hardware engineers access the hardware servers.

The Upgrade Recommendation

You decide to segment your network into the natural clusters of activities. Each segment attached to a port on the Ethernet cross-point switch.

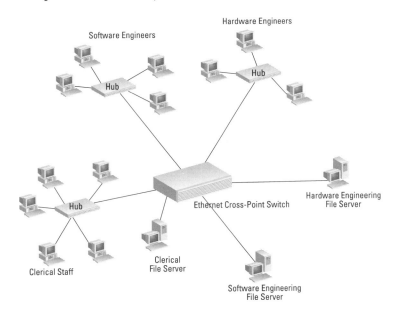

Figure 3-7

You place the clerical staff on one port, and the clerical server on another port; the software engineers on one port of the switch, and the software server on the another port; and the hardware engineers on one port of the switch, and the hardware server on another port.

Reasoning Behind the Recommendation

- **Your performance can be boosted by creating multiple, parallel paths.** Since each user on your network uses one server more than the others, you can get more out of your 10 Mbit/sec network by allowing multiple, parallel conversations on the network. Now, a software engineer can access the software server, a member of the clerical staff can access the clerical server, and a hardware engineer can access the hardware server—all at the same time. However, the cross-point switch will not solve intra-segment traffic congestion. For example, if the software engineers all perform huge file transfers to-and-from the software server), the software segment will still experience network congestion because they all must continue to share the 10 Mbit/sec line. This congestion problem, however, becomes local to that segment—The other segments are not burdened by the software engineer's congestion problem. In this case, you may want to think about installing 100VG-AnyLAN on the software segment to provide a bigger data pipe.

- **No need to update cable infrastructure.** Since Ethernet cross-point switching is still Ethernet, your cable infrastructure is unchanged. To get the most out of your switch, you need to logically group your segments and consciously make a decision on where to place each user.

- **No need to upgrade NICs and hubs.** The only addition to the network is a switch—which makes this a cost-effective method of boosting performance.

4

**Bridging and Routing
Technology and Network
Design**

Bridges and routers can extend your 100VG-AnyLAN network to include 10 Mbit/sec Ethernet, 4 Mbit/sec token ring, 16 Mbit/sec token ring networks, and FDDI networks. You can also use bridges and routers to help control the flow of network traffic on your 100VG-AnyLAN network by selectively filtering packets that cross over the bridge.

For discussion purposes, this chapter assumes a 10 Mbit/sec Ethernet, 4 Mbit/sec token ring or 16 Mbit/sec token ring network. Bridges and routers are common on these types of networks. Bridging and routing concepts, however, hold true for 100VG-AnyLAN networks—and bridges and routers are an important part when adding 100VG-AnyLANs to your existing Ethernet or token ring networks.

Bridges

Bridges can increase the effective bandwidth of your LAN by minimizing network traffic seen by end nodes.

A bridge divides a large LAN into two or more smaller LAN segments and then controls the network traffic between the segments. A bridge identifies nodes on a network by using MAC addresses and an internal address table. When a bridge receives a data packet, it examines the source and destination MAC address and uses its address table to determine how to process the packet. Source addresses are used to build the address tables, and destination addresses are used to router packets. The address table keeps track of where each node is located on each of the connected segments. If the address table shows that the source and destination nodes are on the same segment, then the bridge does not forward the packet to other segments; if the source and destination addresses are on different segments, the packet is forwarded. By discarding packets that do not need to be forwarded, you may realize better network performance.

Bridges operates at the MAC sublayer of the Data Link Layer of the OSI network model. They are invisible to network operating systems and higher level protocols.

Consider the example in figure 4-1. The user on PC 1 wants to copy a file to File Server 1.

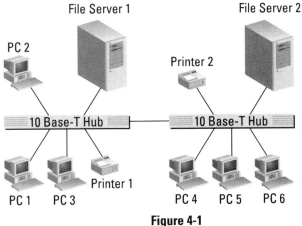

Figure 4-1

PC 1 transmits the file onto the network . All nodes on the entire network (PC 2 - PC 6, File Server 1 and File Server 2, and Printer 1 and Printer 2) must receive the file and initially process it. After initial processing, File Server 1 recognizes its destination address, and processes the packet.

Because all nodes must have access to the file while it is on the network, only one packet can be active on the network at a time—multiple packets cannot simultaneously share the LAN. Shared access networks—such as Ethernet and token ring networks—are bounded by this limitation.

Bridges

Consider installing a bridge on the network as shown in figure 4-2.

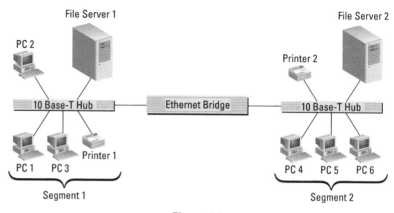

Figure 4-2

The newly added bridge could potentially reduce network traffic by splitting the single segment into two segments and isolating all intra-segment traffic.

Compare the previous scenario— PC 1 wants to copy a file to File Server 1. Since PC1 and File Server 1 are on the same segment (segment 1), the packet will be transmitted to all nodes in segment 1 only. The bridge filters (does not forward) the packet to segment 2. Suppose, at the same time, PC 4 sends a packet to File Server 2. Since PC 4 and File Server 2 are on the same segment (segment 2), the bridge will not forward the packet to segment 1. Both packets can be received by the destination nodes simultaneously since only one packet per segment is active. The bridge has effectively increased the number of simultaneous messages that can be sent on the original LAN from one to two.

Suppose, PC 1 wants to send a file to File Server 2. The bridge will forward the packet to File Server 2—in this case, you have not taken advantage of packet filtering since no other message can exist on the LAN.

As you have seen in the above example, network design plays an important part in determining whether a bridge can boost network performance. To best make use of the filtering capabilities of a bridge, servers and network peripherals shared by a group of clients should be placed on the same side of the bridge as the group of clients accessing them. The advantages of a bridge decrease as more packets cross over the bridge. Substantial inter-segment traffic can overload your bridge, causing network delays. To prevent this, try to limit inter-segment traffic by carefully considering which end nodes should attach to each segment. This process takes time and may need to be regularly reviewed on rapidly growing networks.

Bridging Advantages

Along with potentially adding bandwidth to your network by minimizing excess traffic, bridges may also add these advantages to your network:

- provides security between the networks it connects

- extends a LAN that has reached it configuration limits

- providing redundancy (or fault tolerance) by allowing multiple paths between two bridges.

- provides OSI level 2 (MAC) speed-matching services for LANs that are different speeds but similar packet types

- provides OSI level 2 (MAC) packet translation so two packets with different level 2 packet types can communicate

Network Security

Some bridges allow you to control the accessibility of data on your network.

For example, you may be able to manually enter individual MAC addresses in the bridge's internal address table of only those nodes allowed to communicate across the bridge. Some bridges allow you to add addresses of the nodes that cannot communicate across the bridge. This level of security provides network security not usually associated with shared-access networks.

Extends a LAN

In an Ethernet network, a bridge separates a single-segment LAN into multiple collision domains. Since collisions are not repeated, you can add nodes and add repeaters on networks that have reached configuration limits.

In a token ring network, a bridge separates a large ring into multiple, smaller rings. You can add more nodes and reduce the token delay times with the addition of a bridge.

Provides Redundancy

Many of today's bridges use the spanning tree protocol developed by the IEEE 802.1 committee. The spanning tree protocol allows you to install redundant bridges on the network as backup, while ensuring that only one path at a time is active between any two nodes on the network. In the event that an active path or bridge fails, spanning tree protocol automatically activates an available path through the back up bridge.

OSI Level 2 Translation

You can use a bridge to attach a 100VG-AnyLAN token ring-based network to a 100VG-AnyLAN Ethernet-packet format network because a bridge operates at the data link layer.

You can also use a simple speed-matching bridge when you want to connect two LANs together that differ in speed but are similar in level 3 (and higher) protocols. For example, you can upgrade your 4-Mbit token ring network by adding a 16 Mbit token ring network, and attaching a 4 -to-16 Mbit/sec bridge between the two. Both token ring LANs use the same level three protocols (and in this case, the same level 2 protocols), but differ in speed.

You will also see bridges used in 100VG-AnyLAN networks. You can easily connect your 100VG-AnyLAN to a Ethernet LAN by installing a simple 10:100, speed matching bridge between the two networks.

You can easily connect your 100VG-AnyLAN to a token ring LAN by installing a simple 16:100 speed matching bridge or a 4:100 speed matching bridge between the two networks.

Bridging Limitations

Before adding a bridge to your network, be sure to consider:

High latency potential. Many bridges are considered media-speed—that is, many bridges have the ability to transmit and forward data packets as fast as the physical layer rate. For example, the physical data rate for an IEEE 802.3 Ethernet network is 10 MBit/sec. When data frames appear (at the fastest rate possible) on the networks attached to a bridge, the media-speed bridge is fast enough to process each frame before receiving the next packet. This ensures that the bridge does not become a traffic bottleneck during peak network loading.

Some bridges, however, are incapable of moving continuous, minimum-sized packets. When this happens, the bridge does not perform at media speed—and could be a source of performance degradation. If you have multiple bridges between communicating nodes, the delays could be compounded.

Store-and-forward limitations. A bridge stores and then forwards packets to the appropriate segment. Store-and-forward delays introduced by your bridge may cause network performance degradation.

Ongoing topology analysis to minimize inter-segment traffic. To significantly reduce network traffic and maximize the number of simultaneous packets on the network, you should determine which side of the bridge to place file servers and end nodes. This decision can require benchmarking your network performance using network analysis tools such as network management software and protocol analyzers. And, once this decision is made, you should continue to monitor the network for changing traffic patterns.

Routing

Routers operate at the network layer (layer 3) as defined in the OSI model. A router is an addressable node connecting several types of networks. End nodes send packets directly to the router, which in turn forwards them on the optimal path across the internetwork to their final destination. The routing decision is based on the destination node's network-layer address and other metrics such as the shortest path to a node.

Many routers can also be configured as bridges. If the packet comes into the router, and the router does not recognize the protocol, many routers attempt to bridge the packet.

You can increase network performance with the use of routers by:

- adding a high-speed backbone

- adding a collapsed backbone to your network

- eliminating packets on the network

Adding a High-Speed Backbone

You may be able to increase the performance of your network by adding a high-speed backbone. For example, you can increase throughput by installing a FDDI backbone, which operates at 100 Mbit/sec between one or more LANs, as shown in figure 4-3.

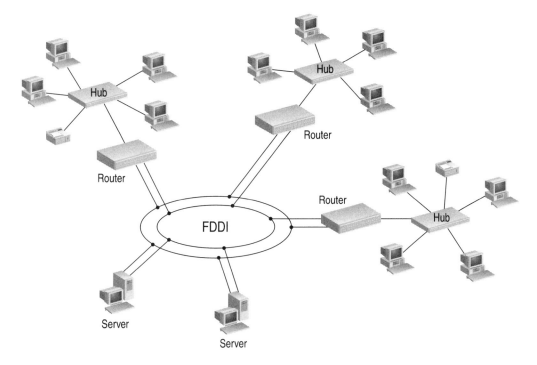

Figure 4-3

Servers can be placed directly on the fiber-optic backbone. Even though the workgroups operate at 10 Mbit/sec, users in workgroup receive responses more rapidly because the backbone is not congested with traffic.

Adding a Collapsed Backbone

A collapsed router backbone takes advantage of your router's high-speed backplane. LAN segments attach to a multi-port router, as shown in figure 4-4.

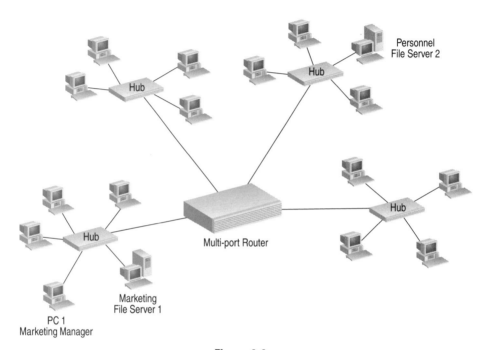

Figure 4-4

For example. one segment of this network consists of the marketing department; anther segment is comprised of the personnel department. Most of the time, the marketing manager remains on the marketing LAN segment. However, today the marketing manager must complete a performance evaluation for one of her engineers—and needs to access the personnel department's data base.

Because the marketing manager's network administrator installed a
collapsed-backbone router with a high-speed backplane, the
marketing manager should not see a degradation in performance
(based on the high level of inter-segment traffic), since the packet
will travel at 2 Gbits/sec (the aggregate speed of the router
backplane) through the router, as shown in figure 4-5.

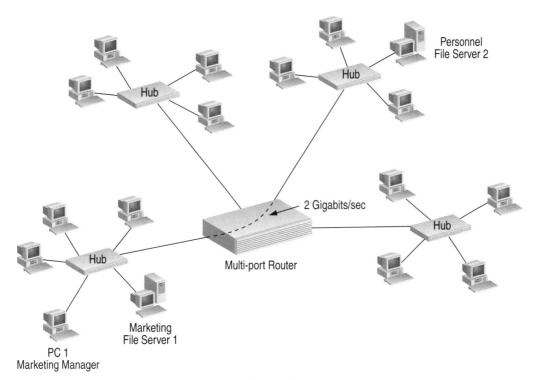

Figure 4-5

Eliminating Packets on the Network

Since routers work at the network layer (layer three of the OSI
model), they drop all MAC layer (layer 2) multicast and broadcast
messages. For example, ARP packets are not passed though the
router.

You can limit layer these broadcast messages by controlling which
network addresses are broadcast.

By eliminating the propagation of broadcast packets, the router can
relieve some network congestion.

Routing Advantages

Adding routers to your network can provide these networking advantages:

- A router provides a firewall between different network segments. You also have great filtering capabilities between one or more segments.

- Routers gives you the flexibility to build your network effectively, tailored to your business—For example, you can control the address scheme of your network.

- You can build security in your networks. A router prevents unknown addresses and devices from entering onto your LAN, providing a level of security not available with a non-routed LAN.

Routing Limitations

Before adding a router to your network, be sure to consider:

- Routers are usually harder to configure, maintain, and troubleshoot than hubs and bridges. For example, many routed networks require you to enter the address of the closest router when you configure an end node device.

- Few routers are network ready. Before configuring a router, you should understand a protocol's addressing scheme. You can control the addressing scheme, and any misconfigured or inefficient addresses can build a poor-performing network.

Updating the Engineering Department

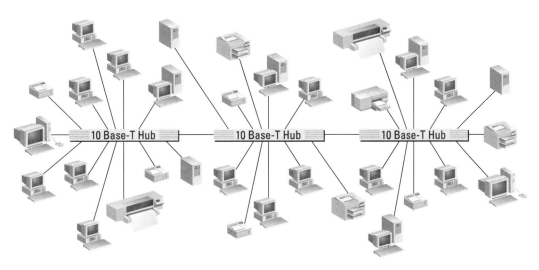

Figure 4-6

Suppose your Ethernet engineering department network is having performance problems. Your current network is a single segmented network, as shown in figure 4-6. After analysis, you find that:

- collisions are extremely frequent on the LAN—causing intermittent connection problems

- traffic patterns indicate that the clerical users use the clerical servers, software engineers use the software servers, and hardware engineers use the hardware servers.

- peer-to-peer networking is on the rise—especially in the engineering departments

- the software engineers are developing a highly confidential project—and software management is concerned about potential security risks

The Upgrade Recommendation

You decide to divide your single-segmented LAN into four segments
and place each of the segments on a port of a multi-port bridge.

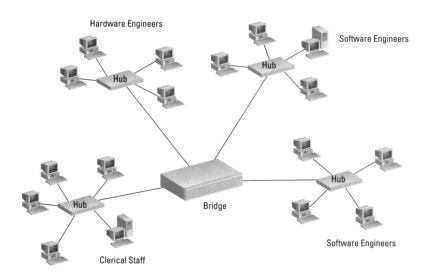

Figure 4-7

Your segments consist of the clerical, hardware, and two software
workgroups. The software engineers on the confidential project are
placed on a single segment. It is very important to try to keep end
users and their servers together on a segment—Inter-segment traffic
defeat the purpose of the bridge.

Reasoning Behind the Recommendation

■ **Performance may be improved by filtering packets so only those packets that need to pass through the bridge do so**. This localizes the traffic on a segment basis—and heavy intra-traffic does not affect the entire LAN.

■ **Protection of investment—No need to purchase additional equipment** (NICs, cabling, etc)

■ **Security is enhanced.** Filtering capabilities allow you to selectively choose whose traffic can pass the bridge. This is especially important for the software group.